SSADM Foundation

Office of Government Commerce

London: TSO

TƧO

Published by TSO (The Stationery Office) and available from:

Online
www.tso.co.uk/bookshop

Mail, Telephone, Fax & E-mail
TSO
PO Box 29, Norwich NR3 1GN
Telephone orders/General enquiries 0870 600 5522
Fax orders: 0870 600 5533
Email: book.orders@tso.co.uk
Textphone: 0870 240 3701

TSO Shops
123 Kingsway, London WC2B 6PQ
020 7242 6393 Fax 020 7242 6394
68-69 Bull Street, Birmingham B4 6AD
0121 236 9696 Fax 0121 236 9699
9-21 Princess Street, Manchester M60 8AS
0161 834 7201 Fax 0161 833 0634
16 Arthur Street, Belfast BT1 4GD
028 9023 8451 Fax 028 9023 5401
18-19 High Street, Cardiff CF10 1PT
029 2039 5548 Fax 029 2038 4347
71 Lothian Road, Edinburgh EH3 9AZ
0870 606 5566 Fax 0870 606 5588

TSO Accredited Agents
(See Yellow Pages)

and through good booksellers

For further information on OGC products, contact:

OGC Service Desk
Rosebery Court
St Andrews Business Park
Norwich NR7 0HS
Telephone + 44 (0) 845 000 4999

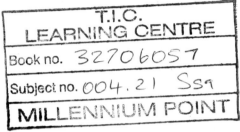

First published 2000
Second impression 2004

ISBN 0 11 330870 1

The OGC is now the authority for best practice in commercial activities in UK Government, combining a number of separate functions with related aims.

OGC will build on the popular guidance developed by the former CCTA and others, working with organisations internationally to develop and share business and practitioner guidance within a world-class best practice framework.

Titles within the Business Systems Development series include:

SSADM Foundation	ISBN 0 11 330870 1
Data Modelling	ISBN 0 11 330871 X
The Business Context	ISBN 0 11 330872 8
User-Centred Design	ISBN 0 11 330873 6
Behaviour and Process Modelling	ISBN 0 11 330874 4
Function Modelling	ISBN 0 11 330875 2
Database and Physical Process Design	ISBN 0 11 330876 0
Also available as a boxed set	ISBN 0 11 330883 3

Printed in the United Kingdom for The Stationery Office
Id 164283 C5 02/04 932910 19585

CONTENTS

FOREWORD

The Business Systems Development (BSD) series represents 'best practice' approaches to investigating, modelling and specifying Information Systems. The techniques described within this series have been used on systems development projects for a number of years and a substantial amount of experience has contributed to the development of this guidance.

Within the BSD series the techniques are organised into groups that cover specific areas of the development process, for example *User Centred Design* which covers all aspects of the investigation, specification and design of the user interface.

The techniques provide a practical approach to the analysis and design of IT systems. They can also be used in conjunction with other complementary techniques such as Object-Oriented techniques.

The material used within this series originated in the Structured Systems Analysis and Design Method (SSADM) which was introduced by the CCTA as a standard method for the development of medium to large IT systems. Since its introduction in the early 1980's, SSADM has been developed through a number of versions to keep pace with the evolving technology and approaches in the IT industry.

The *SSADM Foundation* volume within the BSD series describes the basic concepts of the method and the way in which it can be employed on projects. It also describes how the different techniques can be used in combination. Each of the other volumes in the series describes techniques and approaches for developing elements of the overall specification and design. These can be used in conjunction with one another or as part of alternative approaches. Cross-referencing is provided in outline within the description of each of the techniques to give pointers to the other approaches and techniques that should be considered for use in combination with the one being described.

All volumes within the Business System Development series are available from:

The Stationery Office
St Crispins
Duke Street
Norwich
NR3 1PD

Acknowledgments

Laurence Slater of Slater Consulting Ltd is acknowledged for editing existing material and where necessary developing new material for the volumes within the Business Systems Development series. John Hall, Jennifer Stapleton, Caroline Slater and Ian Clowes are acknowledged for much of the original material on which this series is based.

The following are thanked for their contribution and co-operation in the development of this series:

Paul Turner	-	Parity Training
Tony Jenkins	-	Parity Training
Caroline Slater	-	Slater Consulting Ltd

In addition to those named above a number of people agreed to review aspects of the series and they are thanked accordingly.

1   INTRODUCTION TO THIS VOLUME

The purpose of SSADM (Structured System Analysis and Design Method) is to assist with the development of well engineered systems by employing a number of mature techniques and approaches to produce clear and unambiguous specifications of what is to be developed.

This volume is part of the Business System Development (BSD) series. The other books in the series deal with collections of techniques that can be used together to help with one or more different aspects of the analysis and design of a new system. These techniques can be used together or separately. All the techniques and products which are described in outline in this volume are expanded on in the other volumes.

SSADM, which was originally developed in 1981, shows how all these techniques can be packaged together so that a project 'using SSADM' will be sure that all aspects of analysis and design will be covered. Areas covered by SSADM include:

- analysis of the current business procedures and organisation to see how a new system will best fit into them;
- analysis of any system (automated or manual) that covers the same or similar functions to those for the new system to ascertain how they work and what could be done to improve them;
- analysis and design of the data requirements for the new system including any adhoc reporting required from it;
- analysis and design of the processing required to enable the data to be captured, manipulated, stored and then reported on;
- analysis and design of the interface required to support the user when working with the new system;
- first-cut design for the database of the new system and the physical processes required to access the data.

SSADM has gone through a number of changes since its original publication with the last version being issued in 1996 as 'SSADM 4+ version 4.3'.

In all previous versions the definition of the products and techniques has been tightly integrated into the method. With the publication of the Business System Development series this has changed. This volume contains only an overview of the individual products and techniques required for analysis and design and for more information the appropriate volume will have to be consulted. However, whereas the other volumes deal with only certain elements of analysis and design, this volume does demonstrate how all these techniques and products can be put together to provide a complete method. Within the whole series a single consistent case study (EU-Rent) is used to demonstrate aspects of the techniques and products. For a description of the EU-Rent case study, see Annexe A.

It should be noted that two techniques are regarded as an integral part of SSADM and as such are not covered by the other volumes in this series. These are the decision structure techniques (Business System Options and Technical System Options) in which the user makes decisions firstly about the boundary of and functions to be covered by the new system and then goes on to decide the technical architecture that the new system will be developed on. Both of these techniques are covered in detail within this volume.

SSADM is designed to be customised for individual projects and there is nothing to stop projects or organisations supplementing or replacing products and techniques described here (e.g., using Object Oriented analysis and design techniques). Indeed, this is encouraged where it is to the benefit of the development of the new system. However, a minimum set of fundamental concepts must still be present to enable this to be still called SSADM. For more details see section 9.4 on Customising SSADM.

Organisation of techniques

Within the Business System Development series the techniques are organised into related groups where each of the groups is covered within one volume. This organisation of the techniques is followed within SSADM and is:

- The Business Context
    - Business Activity Modelling
    - Requirements Definition
- Data Modelling
    - Logical Data Modelling
    - Relational Data Analysis
- Function Modelling
    - Data Flow Modelling
    - Function Definition (for off-line functions)
- User Centred Design
    - Work Practice Modelling
    - User Object Modelling
    - Function Definition (for on-line functions)
    - User Interface Design
    - Prototyping and Evaluation
- Behaviour and Process Modelling
    - Entity Behaviour Modelling
    - Conceptual Process Modelling
- Database and Physical Process Design
    - Database Design
    - Physical Process Design

Organisation of this volume

After this (introductory) chapter this volume is organised as follows:

Chapter 2 – Introduction to SSADM. This chapter introduces SSADM in terms of its position within the development lifecycle and introduces the System Development Template, the Product Breakdown Structure and the Default Structural Model.

Chapter 3 – The Business Context. This chapter gives an overview of the concepts, products and techniques covered by the analysis of the business processes which will be assisted by the new system.

Chapter 4 – Data Modelling. This chapter gives an overview of the concepts, products and techniques covered by the analysis and logical design of the data requirements for the new system.

Chapter 5 – Function Modelling. This chapter gives an overview of the concepts, products and techniques covered by the analysis of the data flow for any current system and the design of the data flow for the new system. It also includes the design of the off-line functions.

Chapter 6 – User Centred Design. This chapter gives an overview of the concepts, products and techniques covered by the analysis of the user's requirements for their use of the system and the logical design of the user interface. It also includes the design of the on-line functions.

Chapter 7 – Behaviour and Process Modelling This chapter gives an overview of the concepts, products and techniques covered by the modelling of the behaviour of the entities over time and the logical design of the processing requirements for the new system.

Chapter 8 – Database and Physical Process Design. This chapter gives an overview of the concepts, products and techniques covered by the physical design of the database for the new system and the processes required to access that data.

Chapter 9 – Project Management Considerations. This chapter gives details of project management considerations related to SSADM. Areas covered include the take-on of SSADM by a project/organisation, the management of an SSADM project, the business case for using SSADM as a basis for analysis and design and the customisation of SSADM.

Chapter 10 – Options. This chapter gives a definition of the concepts, products and techniques associated with Business System Options and Technical System Options.

Chapter 11 – Product Breakdown Structure. This chapter gives a Product Breakdown Structure in which all the products for SSADM are organised into groups.

Chapter 12 – Default Structural Model. The Structural Model described in this chapter is a default one defined for SSADM. It shows stages and steps that can then be used to plan, manage and control a project using SSADM.

Annexes. There are two annexes appended to this volume. The first gives a description of EU-Rent which is the case study used throughout this volume.. The second is a glossary of terms that are relevant to this volume.

2   INTRODUCTION TO SSADM

Structured Systems Analysis and Design Method (SSADM) is a comprehensive method containing techniques and products for systems analysis and design. Flexibility is a key feature of SSADM. The elements of the method may be used as rigorously as appropriate. Individual products and techniques may be used, supplemented, varied, replaced or even omitted according to the needs of the specific project, programme or the organisation as a whole.

SSADM was initially introduced, in 1981, as a standard for development projects undertaken within government departments. It was soon adopted by private sector organisations and is currently the development standard in a significant number of public and private organisations both in the UK and worldwide.

2.1   Position of SSADM in the Development Life Cycle

SSADM provides a complete application development framework, a set of product specifications and the associated procedures for undertaking the tasks of systems analysis and design. The format of these specifications enables its use within a properly planned, managed and controlled project. The project management method is not part of SSADM and is not intended as a project management method. It is often used in conjunction with PRINCE2 which is a standard approach to the controlled delivery of projects.

The business context is the starting point for SSADM. Organisations may have already defined wider business planning strategies or established a corporate IS strategy. In this case, the SSADM project must align with the wider objectives defined.

It should be noted that application development projects are essentially linear, albeit with opportunities for iterated and/or parallel tasks. Strategic planning, however, typically follows a one- to five-year cycle of scoping, definition, implementation and review. Figure 2-1 shows these different dimensions.

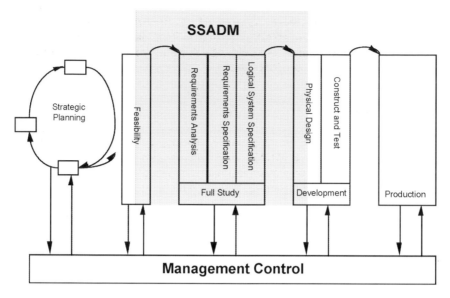

Figure 2-1 Position of SSADM in the Project Life Cycle

The techniques of SSADM fully meet the needs of practitioners for defining functional and information requirements for many types of application. It must be remembered, however, that SSADM is not a panacea to every aspect of implementing IT.

SSADM is not a method for IS Strategy Studies, the scope of which is much broader than that of SSADM. However, some SSADM techniques such as Logical Data Modelling and Business Activity Modelling may be suitable in producing some of the 'models of the business'. SSADM techniques will not identify organisational strengths and weakness, identify critical success factors or business objectives, or identify opportunities.

SSADM can be usefully applied in Feasibility Studies. Here it can help the study team explore the detail of candidate applications and opportunities to use IT in various ways. But even here SSADM is still not the complete answer. Other aspects such as organisational and financial feasibility have to be considered and there are well established techniques to help with this.

A Feasibility Study can be a good key mechanism for providing an applications development project with its terms of reference. Whether such a study is undertaken or not, the analysis team will require a Project Initiation Document (PID) covering the project's objectives, scope and constraints. In SSADM, when the Feasibility Study is initiated, it is assumed that an IT project is required.

An SSADM project provides comprehensive detail about the business requirement for the system. This detail falls into three areas:

- function and data requirements, with objective measures to determine quality;
- a logical design specifying operations to handle business events and enquiry requirements, and the interaction with the user;

- a Technical System Architecture, specifying hardware, software and organisational components to accommodate the system to be implemented. (Some of this specification work may be provided by third-party hardware and software suppliers, depending on contractual procedures).

2.2   SSADM Rationale

SSADM provides a complete framework for capturing and analysing requirements and specifying a system design. SSADM is a flexible, customisable method with an underlying rationale which describes some essential characteristics of the method that must be preserved through any customisation. Preserving these characteristics will ensure that:

- SSADM maintains a quality approach through the close integration between techniques;
- the benefits from using SSADM are realised.

The key components of the SSADM rationale are:

- providing IT support for business activity;
- a 3-schema Specification Architecture, defining the separation of concerns throughout systems development;
- a System Development Template, defining the broad project structure;
- the fundamental concepts of SSADM;
- an approach for defining the scope of the required IT system;
- a Structural Model.

Each of these is explained further in the sections below.

2.2.1 Providing support of the business activity

SSADM is directed at development of IT systems to support business needs. Explicit Business Activity and Work Practice Models should be produced as part of, or as input to, an SSADM project.

SSADM does not mandate a particular method of developing Business Activity and Work Practice Models; there are several methods with which SSADM can work in concert.

Business Activity Model

Whichever method or approach is used, the Business Activity Model should have four parts:

- why the business system exists: the business perspectives that define the motivation for the business and lead to identification of success factors and measures of performance;

- what is done: business activities, the dependencies between them and the resources they use;

- how activities are done: business rules, constraints, calculations, transformations;

- when activities are done: business events that trigger business activities.

A Business Activity Model should be provided as input to the SSADM project, or developed during the early stages of the project.

Work Practice Model

The Work Practice Model is a mapping of the Business Activity Model onto an organisation structure. It specifies:

- who (individual role or organisational unit) is responsible for business activities;

- where business activities are carried out.

A partly specified Work Practice Model may be provided as input to the SSADM project, and completed with detail of how to use the IT system. Alternatively, the Work Practice Model may be developed in parallel with the IT development activities of SSADM.

2.2.2 3-schema Specification Architecture

The 3-schema Specification Architecture is included in the SSADM rationale as a means of understanding the method's structure, in particular the distinction between the modelling of business rules, the user interface and the physical implementation of data management. This separation of concerns helps maintain a degree of independence between the logical business requirements and the system implementation strategy, thus increasing the flexibility and robustness of the system design.

The 3-schema Specification Architecture divides the system design into three areas or 'views'.

Conceptual Model

The Conceptual Model comprises the essential business rules and knowledge. It is a system model which is independent of the user interface and hence is portable between different implementation environments. There is, in some sense, a 'right' answer to Conceptual Model design, in that two analysts who used SSADM on the same problem should come up with conceptual models that are recognisably similar. The Conceptual Model consists of:

- the Logical Data Model;

- enquiry and event processes;

- automated business activities.

External Design

The External Design comprises the user interface:

- data definitions for input/output files;

- window specifications;

- process definitions for window navigation;

- input/output programs.

External Design depends on trade-offs between many factors, for example, ergonomics, system efficiency and users' various subjective preferences. This is a creative area and heuristic approaches, such as prototyping, have a role here.

The External Design passes event data and enquiry triggers to the Conceptual Model, and receives event and enquiry output in response. It has three major elements:

- a packaging of the outputs provided by, and the inputs needed by, the Conceptual Model into functions that serve user roles;

- processing specifications, including processing:
    - to convert inputs from business activities to event data and enquiry triggers;
    - to convert event and enquiry responses to outputs for users;

- a mapping of the External Design's logical specification to a user interface.

Internal Design

The Internal Design defines the physical database design and the process/data interface (PDI). Once again there is a dependency on trade-offs, this time between such factors as timing, space utilisation and maintainability. It is also a creative area where there is no 'right' answer. Heuristic approaches may be appropriate.

2.2.3 Relationship between Business Activities and the 3-schema Specification Architecture

The relationship between the business activities and all three views of the 3-schema Specification Architecture is shown in Figure 2-2.

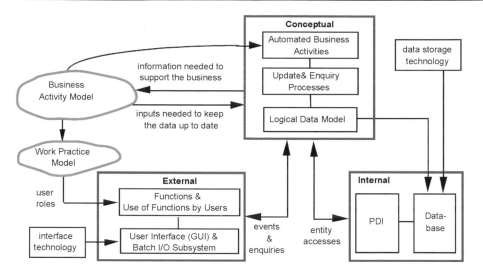

Figure 2-2 Business Activity and the 3-schema Specification Architecture

Ultimately, the processes in each view of the system could be implemented by distinct programs or modules in the implemented system. The Conceptual Model should be portable, or reusable, between different user environments and different physical implementations.

2.3   The System Development Template

The System Development Template (SDT) provides a common structure for the overall system development process. This template is used extensively in the definition of SSADM.

The System Development Template divides the development process into a number of distinct areas of concern, as shown in Figure 2-3 below.

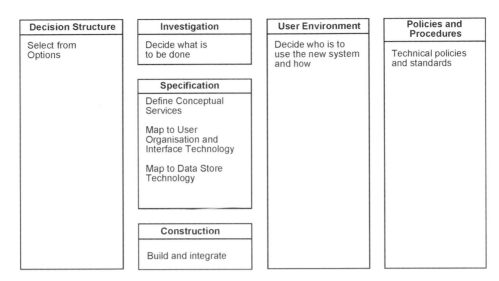

Figure 2-3 System Development Template general view

The 3-schema specification architecture (which covers the Specification area and is described in section 2.2.2 above) concentrates on those products that will ultimately lead, sometimes via other products, into elements of software. The SDT takes a broader view and divides the system development process into activity areas onto which all the development products may be mapped.

Figure 2-4 illustrates the mapping of the full SSADM product set onto the System Development Template. It also shows how products developed in different areas of the development process feed into, or are derived from, each other.

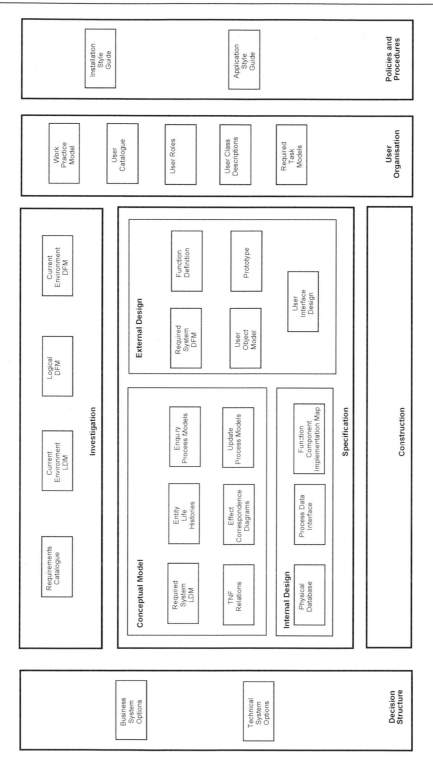

Figure 2-4 Mapping of SSADM products to SDT

2.4   The Default Structural Model

A Structural Model is a kind of 'road map' that enables a project to plan, organise and manage an SSADM project. It breaks the activities involved in the development project into smaller, more manageable chunks of works.

An SSADM Structural Model consists of a number of Modules. Each Module consists of one or more stages. Each stage is described further by a series of steps.

SSADM comprises four Modules as shown in Figure 2-5. These are:

- Requirements Analysis;

- Requirements Specification;

- Logical System Specification;

- Database and Physical Process Design.

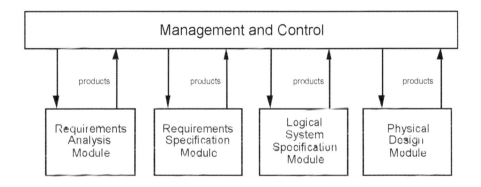

Figure 2-5 SSADM Modules

The techniques and products used within SSADM are applied within the steps. This volume provides a Default Structural Model which should be used as the basis for projects when developing their own structural model, to fit their own project circumstances.

The full Default Structural Model is given in Chapter 12.

It should be noted that the techniques and products present in SSADM can also be used within a Feasibility Study. Generally this will cover those techniques and products from within the Requirements Analysis Module but can also include others if thought useful. Business Systems Options can also be used to decide how best to proceed after the Feasibility Study.

2.5   Product Breakdown Structure

The products of each Module are defined by the SSADM Product Breakdown Structure. Each product is broken down in a hierarchic way, with individual SSADM products at the bottom level of the hierarchy. Some SSADM products appear in several different parts of the Product Breakdown Structure, indicating that versions of the same product are produced in different Modules.

The full Product Breakdown Structure is described in Chapter 11 of this volume.

2.6   Product Descriptions

Each SSADM project should have its own comprehensive set of Product Descriptions which describe the deliverables to be produced. SSADM provides default Product Descriptions which give a comprehensive description of the documentation for all products used throughout the method, and should be used as the basis for defining project-specific Product Descriptions modified to fit with any customisation of the standard SSADM products or to conform with local standards.

Default Product Descriptions can be found at the end of each of the appropriate volumes in this series.

3   THE BUSINESS CONTEXT[1]

Requirements defined for a new automated system will be of a better quality if they are based on knowledge of what users are required to do within the business environment, and what information they need. Requirements definition will be better still if the analyst can understand why the users do what they do, and how different users' business activities are related. This understanding should improve consistency and provide a sound basis for the rest of the project.

IT application projects are mainly focused on the automated information system to be developed. Explicit description of business activities is generally outside their scope; in the development of Data Flow Models, for example, one of the steps is to move manual activity outside the system boundary (where 'system' here means 'automated information system').

It is extremely useful to have an explicit model of business activities, to ensure that requirements to be met by the information system are complete and consistent, and will provide support for coherent user jobs. If there is no explicit model, description of business activities will be spread across a number of analysis and design products with the result that validation of a basic understanding of the business is very difficult.

The Business Context part of an SSADM project is concerned with the modelling of the business within an IT project from which an understanding of requirements is derived. It covers two aspects, these being:

* Business Activity Modelling;

* Requirements Definition.

Business Activity Modelling documents the essential activities that need to be undertaken within the business together with the business events that trigger the activities and the business rules that indicate how an activity is undertaken. This will aid the analyst in understanding how a new system will fit into the overall picture of the business.

Requirements Definition is concerned with documenting requirements for any new IT system.

It should be noted that the concepts, products and techniques described in this volume are concerned with modelling business processes as part of an IT project and not for their own sake. There may be projects undertaken within the organisation which are focused on modelling business processes in order to understand or re-design the way in which the business operates (e.g., a business process re-engineering project). If this is so, these other projects may provide a useful starting point for Business Activity Modelling and Requirements Definition.

---

[1] This chapter contains an overview of the concepts, products and techniques for the business context. For a full description of all the concepts, products, techniques and interrelationships for the business context see, *The Business Context* volume in this series.

3.1   Business Activity Modelling

A Business Activity Model explicitly models what goes on in the business independently of how it will be supported by an information system. Its main purpose is to enable the analyst to identify and document requirements directly from the needs of business activities. This helps to ensure that:

- the degree of subjectivity is reduced such that the new computer system will meet the objectives of the business and not simply re-implement the current system or be constrained by specific perspectives of certain users;

- the design of the IT system will be user centred; the services that the IT system will provide will be designed to support whole user jobs, rather than the IT-system-centred view that a set of enquiries and updates has to be provided, to be used as needed by authorised users.

3.1.1 Concepts for Business Activity Modelling

The following are the main concepts for Business Activity Modelling:

- **Business Perspectives**, which are why the business is doing what it does. When developing IT systems to support business activities, it can be assumed that everyone within the business shares a belief about the basic function of the business. A business perspective is a particular slant on this shared belief. The shared belief can be assumed, but there will be different views about the overall objectives required in order to make the business function in accord with the belief.

- **Business Activities**, which are what the business is doing. Business Activities can be split down into 'doing' activities which are the essential activities of the business, 'enabling' activities which ensure the resources and facilities are available, 'planning' activities which define what needs to be done and 'monitoring' and 'control' activities which check that the other activities are functioning correctly.

- **The Primary Task**, which is a statement of the organisation's mission or objective in the area under investigation.

- **Business Events**, which are triggers for the business activities. Business events are of three types:
  - external inputs;
  - decisions made in business activities;
  - scheduled points of time.

- **Business Rules**, which define how the business activities are done. Rules may be of two types:
  - constraints, which define conditions under which an activity cannot be done or conditions under which an activity must be done;
  - operational guidance, which determines how the activities are done.

3.1.2 Products of Business Activity Modelling

The main product for Business Activity Modelling is the Business Activity Model. This comprises three parts:

- Logical Activity Model;
- Set of Business Events;
- Set of Business Rules.

Logical Activity Model

The Logical Activity Model defines what activities have to be carried out, and the dependencies between them. Five types of activities are identified:

- Doing Activities;
- Enabling Activities;
- Planning Activities;
- Monitoring Activities;
- Controlling Activities.

These should fit the general structure illustrated in Figure 3-1.

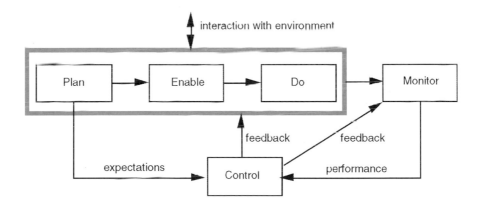

Figure 3-1 Elements of the Logical Activity Model

Set of Business Events

This constitutes the collection of Business Events.

Set of Business Rules

This constitutes the collection of Business Rules.

3.1.3 Interrelationships to other SSADM techniques/products

The following other areas of SSADM are related to Business Activity Modelling:

- **Requirements Definition**, where the Business Activity Model can be used to determine functional requirements. Functional requirements are defined explicitly in terms of information support for business activities. Non-functional requirements may be derived from the measures of performance specified in the Business Activity Model.

- **Data Flow Modelling**, where Business Activity Modelling influences the role of the Current Physical Data Flow Model. The use of Current Physical Data Flow Models allows the analyst to understand the detail of what is currently happening in the area under investigation and provides a means of checking with the user what data is being used and what processes are being performed. This model then needs to be 'logicalised' to establish the underlying functional model. It can be difficult for the analyst to take an objective view of the underlying data and processes during logicalisation as this requires a complete switch in thinking. The development of a Business Activity Model approaches the system from an entirely different viewpoint and allows the analyst to model the essential activities of the system without becoming too involved in the detail of what is actually going on. These two different views are both very useful and can be used to complement one another in the investigation of the system.

- **Logical Data Modelling**, where the requirements for information support to the Business Activity Model will provide a direct set of requirements for the Logical Data Model. Initially, the Business Activity Model will help to identify the data that should be covered in the Current Environment Logical Data Model and later will help to identify data that is needed in the Required System Logical Data Model. The Business Activity Model for a project will have a defined scope within a broader business picture. There may be a corporate data model to support this broader view of the business, with which the project Logical Data Model must be reconciled.

- **Work Practice Modelling**, where the Work Practice Model is a mapping of the Business Activity Model onto an organisation to specify who (which user roles) carries out each business activity and where the activities are carried out.

- **Entity Behaviour Modelling**, where when the information support that is required to support the Business Activity Model has been investigated, it should be possible to identify the way in which the Business Events cause the Logical Data Model to be updated and identify which business activities can provide the inputs.

3.2   Requirements Definition

Requirements Definition establishes functional and non-functional requirements for the proposed system. Its objectives are to:

- identify requirements for the proposed system which meet the needs of users, and of the business as a whole;

- describe requirements in quantifiable terms;
- provide a basis for decisions about the new system;
- ensure analysis is focused on requirements for the future system;
- provide a basis for acceptance criteria.

Requirements Definition is iterative, addressing requirements in increasing detail as the project progresses. Deciding how much detail is required at any given point is a matter of judgement rather than formal technique.

Requirements should always be described in terms which:

- can be measured;
- are detailed enough to reduce ambiguity and to base decisions on;
- minimise duplication across the various specification products;
- can be tested against and thus usable as acceptance criteria.

3.2.1 Concepts of Requirements Definition

The following are the main concepts for Requirements Definition:

- **Functional Requirements**, which are those for facilities and features needed to satisfy the information needs of the user. Basically they cover 'what' the system should do. Types of functional requirements are updates, enquiries, reports and interactions with other systems.
- **Non-Functional Requirements,** which describe how well the new system should work. Types of non-functional requirements include service level requirements, usability, access restrictions, security, monitoring, audit and control, conversion from current system, interfaces with other systems and archiving.

3.2.2 Products of Requirements Definition

The main product of Requirements Definition is the Requirements Catalogue.

The Requirements Catalogue is the central repository for information about requirements and provides a flexible tool for recording and tracking requirements. It is created at the start of Requirements Analysis, or may be provided from an earlier Feasibility Study. Initially, requirements might be recorded only in general terms in the Requirements Catalogue. As the project progresses, the Requirements Catalogue is extended and refined as new requirements are identified and more detail is added.

As the project progresses further, the Requirements Catalogue may grow too large to handle as a single product. It may have to be structured into smaller units based, for example, on business areas or sub-systems.

Ideally, the Requirements Catalogue should be a view of the repository used by the project's CASE tool(s), so that its requirements can then be traced through to solutions via automatic links to specification and design products. If this level of automated support is not available, the Requirements Catalogue is often maintained on a word processor, and cross references between its entries and CASE repository items maintained manually.

3.2.3 Interrelationships to other SSADM techniques/products

Requirements Definition has links with most of the other SSADM techniques and products in that it documents the basic requirements which these other products must be designed to cover. The following are the major areas of SSADM that are related to Requirements Definition:

- **Business Activity Modelling**, which is a major source of requirements.

- **Work Practice Modelling**, where the scope for changing user roles is an important factor in Requirements Definition and Work Practice Modelling.

- **Data Flow Modelling**, where modelling the current environment using Data Flow Diagrams (DFDs) can help identify requirements arising from current problems. The Required System Data Flow Model describes required functionality.

- **Function Definition**. The Requirements Catalogue will identify requirements for enquiries and updates. Function Definition takes these requirements and defines them more rigorously by beginning to define the processing required to support them.

- **Logical Data Modelling.** During Requirements Definition, new requirements may be identified which need additional data items, entities and relationships. Such requirements should be recorded in the Requirements Catalogue and subsequently modelled using the Logical Data Modelling technique. The Required System Logical Data Model ensures the system will be able to support the data requirements of users.

- **Business System Options** where the Requirements Catalogue feeds into the process of defining and selecting Business System Options, indicating functional requirements, priorities and expected benefits for the new system (full details of non-functional requirements are not essential although broad constraints, security requirements, etc., should be available).

- **Technical System Options**. As part of the Requirements Specification, the Requirements Catalogue feeds into the process of defining Technical System Options. System-wide features, constraints and other requirements for the technical environment are considered in the definition of Technical System Options.

4   DATA MODELLING[2]

Data Modelling is at the very heart of any project and does exactly what its name implies –
it models data without concern for the processing that must be applied to maintain the data.

Within SSADM two specific areas of data modelling are covered:

- Production of the Logical Data Model(s);

- Relational Data Analysis.

The main Logical Data Model (LDM) which would be expected to be developed on every
SSADM project is the *Required System Logical Data Model* which models how the data
will be organised in the new system taking into account any current system and all new
requirements. Relational Data Analysis (RDA) can be used to validate this model against
known requirements. The Required System Logical Data Model is the data model which
will go forward to Database Design and which will be maintained throughout the lifetime
of the system.

A Logical Data Model for the current system can be produced on a project if this is
considered helpful. This is the *Current Environment Logical Data Model* which shows the
way data is organised in any current system (either computer or automated).

4.1   Logical Data Modelling

4.1.1 Concepts for Logical Data Modelling

The following are the main concepts for Logical Data Modelling:

- **Entity**, which is an object or concept, either concrete or abstract, that is of
  importance to the area of business being investigated;

- **Relationship**, which is a direct association between two entities or between the
  entity and itself to which all occurrences of the entity must conform. These can be
  of three different kinds one-to-many (1:m), one-to-one (1:1) and many-to-many
  (m:n);

- **Keys**, which are used to identify entity occurrences and to enforce uniqueness of
  the entity occurrences;

- **Attribute**, which is a characteristic of an entity, that is any detail that serves to
  describe, qualify, identify, classify, quantify or express the state of an entity. Each
  attribute is a characteristic of one and only one entity unless it has different roles

---

[2] This chapter contains an overview of the concepts, products and techniques for data modelling.
For a full description of all the concepts, products, techniques and interrelationships for data
modelling, see the *Data Modelling* volume in this series.

within that entity, or appears as part of the key structure for that entity. Thus, attributes can appear in more than one entity only if they are part of the primary key or foreign key or assume several different roles within the same entity;

- **Entity Aspects**, which are used where it is required that an entity is modelled within two or more separate sub-systems;

- **Entity Sub-type/Super-type**, which are used either by several entites being found to have common identifiers or a single entity which has several different and distinct behaviours which are alternatives for one another.

4.1.2 Products of Logical Data Modelling

The main product of Logical Data Modelling is the Logical Data Model. This comprises three parts:

- Logical Data Structure (LDS);

- Entity Descriptions;

- Relationship Descriptions.

Two different Logical Data Models may be produced:

- **Required System Logical Data Model,** to provide a detailed description of the information requirements of the new system. Within SSADM the Required System Logical Data Model should be regarded as a mandatory product;

- **Current Environment Logical Data Model**, to provide a description of the information used or produced by the current environment.

If required, items of data or data types can be centrally defined in a Data Catalogue.

Logical Data Structure

The Logical Data Structure is a diagram showing the entities for the system and the relationships between them.

An example of a Logical Data Structure is in Figure 4-1.

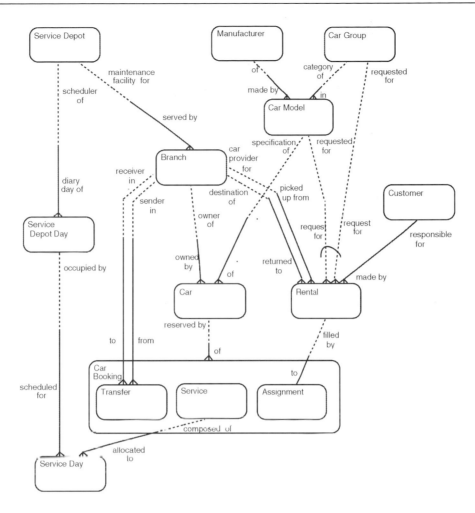

Figure 4-1 Example Logical Data Structure

In the diagram above:

- Entities are represented by boxes;

- Relationships are represented by lines which are either solid (indicating a mandatory relationship) or dotted (indicating an optional relationship). Each relationship can combine both mandatory and optional elements;

- Each crow's foot represents the many end of a one-to-many relationship;

- The box labelled Car Booking (surrounding the entities Transfer, Service and Assignment) shows an example of a super-type;

- The curved line over two of the relationships coming out of the entity Rental shows that these relationships are mutually exclusive;

- The words on the relationships are present to aid with understanding the relationships.

Please note that for a full description of the diagrammatic techniques represented on a Logical Data Model, see the *Data Modelling* volume in this series.

Entity Descriptions

An Entity Description records information about the important characteristics of an entity on the Logical Data Structure.

Relationship Descriptions

A Relationship Description records information about the relationships on the Logical Data Structure. Generally, the majority of information that is required about each relationship appears on the Logical Data Structure itself. However, there may be a requirement to record more precise volumetric information about a relationship or access/security information about the relationship. In this case, a Relationship Description can be produced.

4.1.3 Interrelationships to other SSADM techniques/products

Products that validate the Logical Data Model

A number of the other SSADM products can be used to help validate the Logical Data Model. Chief among these are as follows:

- **Data Flow Model**. Each entity on the Required System Logical Data Model should be contained within one main data store on the Required System Data Flow Model. In addition, the attributes within the entities can be compared with the data items into and out of processes on the Data Flow Model.

- **Business Activity Model**. The Business Activity Model will contain requirements for data outputs from the new system. These should be capable of being satisfied by the entities/attributes in the Required System Logical Data Model.

- **Requirements Catalogue**. The requirements catalogue will contain requirements for data (both to entered into and got out of the new system). The Required System Logical Data Model needs to be capable of satisfying these requirements.

- **Entity Life Histories**. The Entity Life Histories are a detailed analysis of the life of each entity. These are used to validate that the correct entities and attributes have been defined on the Required System Logical Data Model.

In addition to these products, the technique of Relational Data Analysis is used to validate the Logical Data Model (see below).

Relationships with other SSADM techniques and products

The following areas of SSADM utilise the Logical Data Model:

- **Entity Life Histories**. One Entity Life History is developed for each of the entites on the Required System Logical Data Model;

- **Enquiry Access Paths and Effect Correspondence Diagrams.** The Enquiry Access Paths and Effect Correspondence diagrams show navigation around the Required System Logical Data Model;

- **Database Design**. The database design for the new system should primarily be based upon the Required System Logical Data Model.

Within Business Systems Options, Logical Data Models may be produced to help define the scope for each of the Business System Options.

4.2   Relational Data Analysis

Relational Data Analysis in SSADM is a complement and a check to Logical Data Modelling. The purpose of Relational Data Analysis (RDA) is to:

- capture the user's detailed knowledge of the meaning and significance of the data;

- validate the Logical Data Model by checking that all the required data is present and is structured correctly;

- ensure the data is logically easy to maintain and extend:

  - ensure all data interdependencies have been identified;

  - ensure all ambiguities have been resolved;

  - eliminate unnecessary duplication of data.

- form the data into optimum groups to provide a basis for sharing data between different areas of the application.

Relational Data Analysis helps to check that the Logical Data Model can actually be built and maintained and that all attributes are fully defined. This is done by:

- analysing the inputs and outputs and decomposing them into normalised relations;

- building sub-models from groups of relations, using the keys of the relations to define relationships between them;

- mapping the sub-models onto the Logical Data Model and resolving any differences.

4.2.1 Concepts for Relational Data Analysis

The following are the main concepts for Relational Data Analysis:

- **Relations**, which is defined as being a two-dimensional table; that is, it comprises a number of rows and a number of columns and is equivalent to an entity;

- **Normalisation**, which is the process of producing the optimum grouping of attributes in relations;

- **Primary Key**. Every relation must have a primary key, a non-changeable attribute (or group of non-changeable attributes) whose values uniquely identify rows of the relation;

- **Candidate Key,** which is any (minimal) set of one or more attributes that can for all time be used as such a unique identifier;

- **Foreign Key**, which is defined as a non-key attribute (or group of related non-key attributes) in one relation which is the same as the key of another relation.

4.2.2 Products for Relational Data Analysis

The product that is used to help support the activities of Relational Data Analysis is the Relational Data Analysis Working Paper. From this a model is constructed which is then used to validate the Logical Data Model.

The result of undertaking Relational Data Analysis is that the Required System Logical Data Structure is validated against the data that is input to and output from the system and updated where necessary. As such there are no 'lasting' products from Relational Data Analysis – all products being regarded as transient.

4.2.3 Interrelationships to other SSADM techniques/products

Logical Data Modelling

Relational Data Analysis is a complementary technique to Logical Data Modelling and supports it as a supplementary approach to identifying and specifying information requirements.

Entity analysis derives a Logical Data Model in a top-down manner by a process of decomposition, whereas Relational Data Analysis derives a data model in a bottom-up manner by synthesising individual data items into larger data groups.

The benefits of the two data analysis techniques in combination are as follows:

- Logical Data Modelling, working essentially from the top down, ensures that the overall perception of what is important to the project in terms of data is not lost;

- Relational Data Analysis, working essentially from the bottom up, ensures that all the low-level detail is captured.

Products that provide inputs to Relational Data Analysis

Although the inputs that are used for Relational Data Analysis tend to be derived directly from the users there are a number of other SSADM products that can be used as well. These are:

- **Data Flow Model**, where the I/O Descriptions can be used;

- **I/O Structures**, which are developed as part of modelling of off-line functions;

- **User Object Models**, which show the user's view of how data should be grouped.

5   FUNCTION MODELLING[3]

Function Modelling is concerned with the analysis of the data and process (Data Flow Modelling) within the system and the definition of the required system processing (Data Flow Modelling) and off-line functions (Function Definition).

With Data Flow Modelling the analyst can document the way in which data is processed in any current system and demonstrate the way it will be processed in the system that is to be developed. Once that has been completed the analyst can then use the data flow model to help identify those units of processing (known as functions) which will be developed. Although Data Flow Modelling will assist the user in identification of all functions, within this volume only the derivation of off-line functions will be covered (i.e., those functions which require no user intervention). On-line functions (those that contain some element of user interaction) are covered by User Centred Design (see Chapter 6).

The use of Data Flow Modelling will assist the analyst in a number of ways:

- to clearly identify and document the scope of the new system;

- to document the way in which the processing elements of the system transform data entering the system into data which is output from and stored within the system. This can include both the system that is to be developed and also any existing system;

- to demonstrate to the users of the system that the analyst has a grasp of what the system is required to do and what any current system does.

The use of Function Definition is fundamental to the development of the new system in that it defines the individual units of processing that will be carried forward to design and development of the new system. In addition, Function Definition:

- helps to pull together the different analysis and design products;

- helps in the planning of the development of the new system;

- provides a basis for the sizing of the new system.

5.1   Data Flow Modelling

Data Flow Modelling is used to investigate the flow of data around a system:

- to and from agents external to the system;

- to and from processes which transform the data;

- into and out of repositories or stores of data.

---

[3] This chapter contains an overview of the concepts, products and techniques for function modelling. For a full description of all the concepts, products, techniques and interrelationships for function modelling, see the *Function Modelling* volume in this series.

The technique can be used to model a physical system or a logical abstraction of that system.

Data Flow Modelling has several main purposes:

- to identify and clearly define the scope and boundary of the system and its various components;

- to identify requirements for the new system;

- to help in the identification of events and functions;

- to assist in communications between analyst and user;

- to act as the basis for subsequent design.

Three different Data Flow Models can be produced during a development project. These are:

- **Current Physical Data Flow Model**, which represents the existing system as it is currently implemented;

- **Logical Data Flow Model**, which represents the current system without any physical constraints;

- **Required System Data Flow Model**, which represents a logical view of the new system without any physical constraints and structured around the user's view of the system.

It is the last of these models (Required System Data Flow Model) which is considered the most important in that it represents a view of the system that will be developed and as such will provide a basis for the identification and development of other analysis and design products (e.g., functions and events). The first two models, which are both a view of any existing system, are most of use where there is a requirement for the new system to be similar to an existing one (either automated or manual). This is most likely where the system's operation is covered by law or where the business processes are defined and unchangeable.

5.1.1 *The concepts of Data Flow Modelling*

Data Flow Modelling involves the development of Data Flow Diagrams which are diagrams which are made up of a number of different types of symbols. The basic types of symbols are shown in Figure 5-1 and are further explained in the subsequent paragraphs.

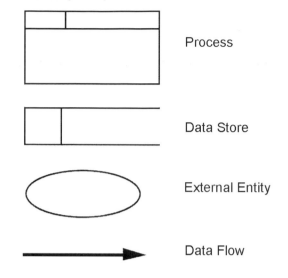

Figure 5-1 Basic concepts of Data Flow Modelling

Process

A process transforms or manipulates data in a system. Each process on a Data Flow Diagram may be broken down into another lower level diagram of several processes.

Data Store

A data store represents a repository of data inside the system boundary. If there is a current system, the data store represents a physical repository of data: a computer file or a manual means of storing data, a box file or card index for instance. On both Logical and Required System Data Flow Diagrams data stores have no suggestion of the physical means of storage but on the Required System Data Flow Model they will probably be implemented in the form of a computer database.

External Entity

An external entity is a source or recipient (or both) of data in the system, and exists outside the boundary of the system. It may be a user of the system, a person or organisation outside the system, or another system.

Data Flow

A data flow represents the flow of information between a process and either a data store, an external entity or another process.

5.1.2 Products of Data Flow Modelling

The main product of Data Flow Modelling is the Data Flow Model. The Data Flow Model is composed of four products:

- Data Flow Diagrams – Level 1 and Lower Levels;
- Elementary Process Descriptions;
- I/O Descriptions;
- External Entity Descriptions.

As mentioned earlier, three variants of the Data Flow Model can exist:

- Current Physical Data Flow Model;
- Logical Data Flow Model;
- Required System Data Flow Model.

In addition to the products covered by these three variants of the Data Flow Model, there are a number of products covered by the Data Flow Modelling technique, each of which falls into one of the following categories:

- intermediate products which are developed as an input to the Data Flow Model and are then usually discarded (Resource Flow Diagram, Document Flow Diagram, Process/Entity Matrix, Logical/Physical Data Store Cross-reference);
- products developed to cross-reference the Data Flow Model with other products (Logical Data Store/Entity Cross-reference);
- products which can use the Data Flow Modelling notations to fulfil a specific need within the project (Overview Data Flow Diagram, Data Flow Diagrams included in Business System Options, Context Diagram).

Products in the first category can be considered as being part of the practice of the technique and are therefore described in detail in this section. The Overview Data Flow Diagram and Business Systems Options Data Flow Diagrams follow the same conventions as the other Data Flow Diagrams so will not be described separately.

The dependencies between all the products mentioned above are shown in Figure 5-2.

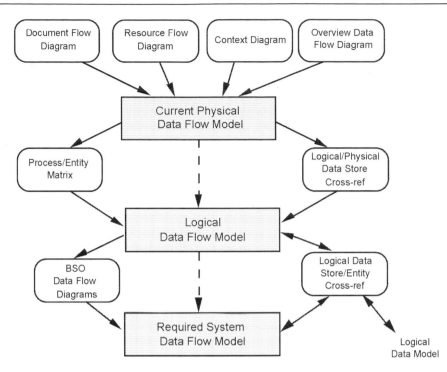

Figure 5-2 Data Flow Modelling Products

The dependencies shown on this diagram are the most common dependencies and should not be taken to be mandatory. For example, where a Business Activity Model is developed, there may be no need to develop a Current Physical Data Flow Model in which case the main input to the Logical Data Flow Model will be the Business Activity Model. Where there is no current system, the Business Activity Model will feed directly into the Required System Data Flow Model.

Data Flow Diagrams (DFDs)

A set of Data Flow Diagrams comprises a Level 1 Data Flow Diagram and Lower Level Diagrams forming a hierarchy to two or three lower levels. A Level 1 Data Flow Diagram represents the whole system on one diagram. Areas of the Level 1 Data Flow Diagram are decomposed to show successively more detail in the lower level Data Flow Diagrams.

Each diagram shows a combination of processes, data stores, external entities and data flows.

An example of a Data Flow Diagram is shown in Figure 5-3.

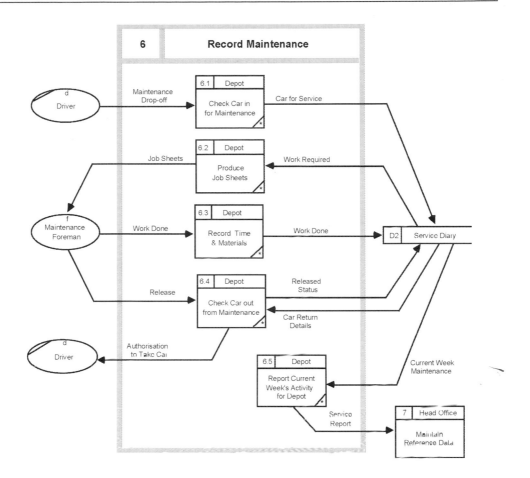

Figure 5-3 Example of Data Flow Diagram

Elementary Process Descriptions

Each process at the lowest level of decomposition is described by an Elementary Process Description (EPD) which is a brief textual description of the process. This description may contain what business constraints dictate how the process is carried out, circumstances under which the process is invoked, constraints on when and by whom the process can be invoked and what data is accessed.

External Entity Descriptions

This is where the analyst records here any relevant detail about the external entity and possible constraints on how it interfaces or is required to interface to the system.

Input/Output Descriptions (I/O Descriptions)

I/O Descriptions describe data flows crossing the system boundary, listing the data items contained in the data flow. Detail of the structure of the data – such as repeating groups and optionality – need not be included, since this will be rigorously defined later during Function Definition.

5.1.3 Interrelationships to other SSADM techniques/products

The following other areas of SSADM are related to Data Flow Modelling:

- **Logical Data Modelling**. The Data Flow Model is developed in parallel with the Logical Data Model, so the two models must be kept consistent with each other. The Current Physical Data Flow Model is developed in parallel with the Current Environment Logical Data Model (LDM) and the Required System Logical Data Model in parallel with the Required Logical Data Model. The analyst must ensure that data in the Logical Data Model entities is represented in data stores and input data flows in the Data Flow Model. This correspondence is done formally when logical data stores are identified by grouping the entities of the Logical Data Structure and the correspondence documented in the Logical Data Store/Entity Cross-reference.

- **Business Activity Modelling**, in that it influences the role of the Current Physical Data Flow Model as they are both modelling the same business system. The use of Current Physical Data Flow Models allows the analyst to understand the detail of what is currently happening in the area under investigation and provides a means of checking with the user what data is being used and what processes are being performed. However, it often causes problems when the analyst is required to take an objective view of the underlying data and processes during logicalisation as this requires a complete switch in thinking. The development of a Business Activity Model approaches the system from an entirely different viewpoint and allows the analyst to model the essential activities of the system without becoming too involved in the detail of what is actually going on. These two different views are both very useful and can be used to complement one another in the investigation of the system.

- **Requirements Definition**. The analyst must ensure that the requirements given in the Requirements Catalogue and confirmed in Business System Options can be supported by the inputs, outputs, data entities and functionality represented in the Data Flow Model.

- **Function Definition**, in that the objective of constructing the Required Data Flow Model is to facilitate Function Definition. The Required System Data Flow Model can be modified where required if new events and functions are not supported by the inputs, processes and updates of data already shown.

- **Entity Behaviour Modelling** where events may be identified from the Required System Data Flow Model with reference to updates to main data stores.

- **User Centred Design** where external entities may be used to identify the system users.

5.2   Function Definition

Function Definition identifies units of processing specification, or functions, which need to be controlled as a whole in order to support the users' tasks.

During the development project two types of function are identified;

- **On-line functions**, where the user interfaces directly with the system either to update some of the information stored within the system or to retrieve information stored by the system or, more normally, a combination of the two;

- **Off-line functions**, where the system operates without user intervention (e.g., back-up). This type of function is sometimes known as a Batch function.

This section deals solely with off-line functions. On-line functions are described as part User Centred Design which is covered in Chapter 6.

5.2.1 Purposes of Function Definition

Function Definition has several purposes:

- it identifies and defines the units of processing specification required to support user tasks which need to be carried forward to physical design;

- it pulls together the products of analysis and design, which together specify a function;

- it develops and confirms a common understanding between the analyst and the user of how the system processing is to be organised;

- it provides a basis for sizing and for deriving design objectives.

A function is a unit of off-line processing which is required to be controlled as a unit in support of a single task. Where the task requires several units of off-line processing which do not directly interact, and do not need to be controlled together, there will be more than one function defined for that task.

5.2.2 Products of Function Definition

The main product of the Function Definition technique is the Function Description. If thought useful this can be supplemented by a I/O Structure which documents the input and output data streams for the function.

Function Description

A Function Description contains some descriptive text and a large number of cross-references to other products.

I/O Structure

I/O Structures (which will only be developed if thought useful), consist of:

- **I/O Structure Diagrams** which are a pictorial representation of the data items that are input to a function and output from a function;

- **I/O Structure Element Descriptions** which are the backing documentation for an I/O Structure Diagram and list the data items represented by each element of the I/O Structure Diagram.

5.2.3 Interrelationships to other SSADM techniques/products

The following other areas of SSADM are related to Function Definition:

- **Entity Behaviour Modelling**, in that the identification of functions often identifies the need for events and enquiries. Conversely, the examination of events and enquiries may help to determine what functions are required.

- **Requirements Definition**, where requirements for enquiries are likely to be documented in the Requirements Catalogue. These enquiry requirements are developed into enquiries which are used by functions or components of functions.

- **Technical System Options**. Function frequency is recorded in the Function Description. This information is useful in the estimation of system sizing and can be input to the formulation of Technical System Options.

6   USER CENTRED DESIGN[4]

Within SSADM, User Centred Design is concerned with the design of the new system from the user's perspective. It includes techniques that can be used as part of investigation to gather details of the way the users are organised within the business and others that can be used as part of the specification of the new system to document the way the new system will look from the user's perspective.

The ultimate aim of this part of the development life cycle is the define the on-line IT processes that the system will need to implement and to define the user interface necessary to support these processes. In a traditional development the outputs from Function Definition provide the first area whilst the outputs from User Interface Design provide the second. As the tools for incremental development have increased over recent years, so has the idea that a system can be developed incrementally using prototyping techniques as the main driver. The advent of new technologies (e.g., e-commerce and electronic mail) have made this method of development more prevalent as it is seen that this way of working produces systems more quickly. Even in these systems it is important that the system built is the correct one and that the interface is a 'friendly' one. To achieve this it is necessary that some formality must be brought to the prototyping.

Five techniques are covered within this subject. These are:

- **Work Practice Modelling**, which examines the way the users are organised within the business and maps then to the Business Activity Model in order to identify tasks;

- **User Object Modelling**, which develops a model of the way the user views the new system in terms of the business processes, the information to be used by the business and the way in which it will be processed;

- **Function Definition**, which defines the processing that will be required to be automated in the new system for the on-line parts of the system;

- **User Interface Design**, which defines the windows which the user will require to use to access and modify the data within the new system. It also defines the way the individual windows will be navigated;

- **Prototyping and Evaluation**, in which views of the new system are developed which can be demonstrated to the users so that basic requirements and features can be discussed with the users. Some prototypes are used as part of the incremental development of the system.

Figure 6-1 shows the relationships between the individual techniques.

---

[4] This chapter contains an overview of the concepts, products and techniques for user centred design. For a full description of all the concepts, products, techniques and interrelationships for the user centred design, see the *User Centred Design* volume in this series.

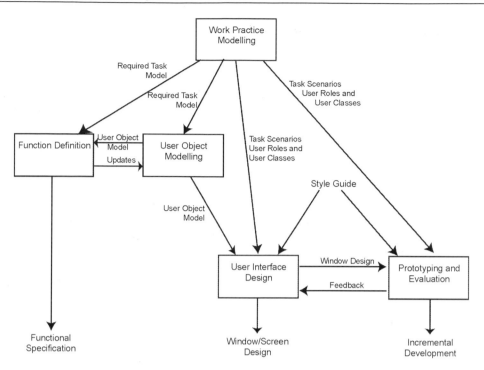

Figure 6-1 User Centred Design techniques

How many of the techniques a project uses – and the tailoring of them – will depend upon the depth of analysis and design the project wishes to go to. Obviously if screen design is the only desired aim of User Centred Design then User Interface Design is the minimum, and if an incremental build is the aim then Prototyping and Evaluation is the minimum.

6.1   Work Practice Modelling

Work Practice Modelling outlines who does what and where within the new system based on the business activities identified and the proposed user organisation. The Work Practice Model is a mapping of the Business Activity Model onto the 'actors' within the organisation structure specified for the business area in which the new system will reside.

The overriding consideration in the approach adopted for Work Practice Modelling is that projects should take account of the complete picture of the business and not just concentrate on the automated system. The automated system must be designed to fit the business needs, not the other way round.

6.1.1 Concepts of Work Practice Modelling

The main concepts for Work Practice Modelling are:

- **Actors,** who can be identified as a collection of proposed job holders who will share a large proportion of common tasks, whether using the IT system or not;

- **Basic Task**, which defined as the complete set of business activities triggered by a single business event irrespective of who or what is to perform the business activities;

- **Task**, which is a human activity performed by an actor or user role in response to a business event. The task is identified with reference to all the business activities triggered by a specific business event which are undertaken by a single actor or user role. Tasks are identified from the 'human' perspective. Many tasks will not involve direct interaction with the automated system. Within a single task there may be some sub-tasks that require interaction with the automated system and other sub-tasks that do not. Tasks that require interaction with the automated system are used to derive the User Object Model and functions;

- **Task Scenario,** which is a concrete example of a specific task which provides a complete story;

- **User,** who is a person who will require direct interaction with the automated system;

- **User roles,** who are the subset of actors who require a user interface to the automated system;

- **User Class,** which is a subset of the total population of users of the required system who are similar in terms of their frequency of use, relevant knowledge and personal experience. A user class is a category of users who have similar personal characteristics and capabilities.

6.1.2 Products of Work Practice Modelling

The main products for Work Practice Modelling are:

- Required Task Models;

- Set of Task Scenarios;

- User Catalogue;

- User Class Description;

- Set of User Roles.

Each of these is described below.

Required Task Models

The complete set of Required Task Models describes all of the human activities and task sequences required by the business system. The Required Task Models elaborate the tasks identified by the mapping of business activities onto the user organisation. Required Task Models cover all of the main task areas and some of the less common tasks.

A Required Task Model is a hierarchical model of a task. It consists of a Task Model Structure and one or more Task Descriptions. At the top level, a task is identified as a set of business activities undertaken by a single actor or user role in response to a business event.

An example of a Task Model in shown in Figure 6-2.

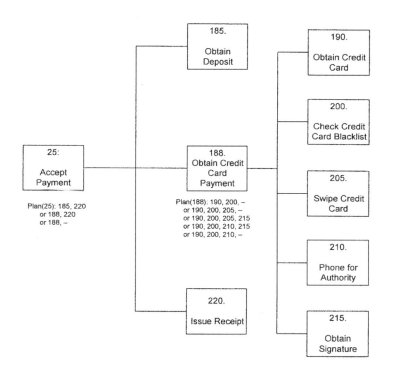

Figure 6-2 Example Task Model

Set of Task Scenarios

A Task Scenario is a concrete example of a specific path through a task. Each Task Scenario describes the actions that a user will perform in using the system to achieve a goal or respond to a specific example of a business event. It can be written in the form of a story or a script. Each Task Scenario consists of a textual description of the scenario including inputs, background and the way in which the tasks are performed. Sub-tasks performed by the system should be distinguished from sub-tasks performed by the user where this split can be identified. It can be written in the form of a story or a script. The scenario should be annotated to indicate whether this is a typical scenario or likely to be an exception.

User Catalogue

The User Catalogue is a description of the target users and the task areas they undertake. A User Catalogue can be initiated based on the users of the current system provided there is minimal restructuring anticipated. Its main focus should be on recording details of users and tasks necessary for the required system. The purpose of the User Catalogue is to assist in the identification of user roles from actors.

User Class Descriptions

User Class Descriptions are an optional product that would normally only be produced when there is a large and diverse user population. A User Class Description can be used to provide a detailed description of a category of user which is used to determine the requirements for the style and general features of the user interface design.

Set of User Roles

User roles are those actors who will require direct access to the automated system within the business system. The identification of user roles allows individuals to adopt different roles in different circumstances. This is rationalising users based on their need to access common functions. Conversely, if two sets of users share similar tasks but one set is permitted access to different sets of data from the other, it is necessary to identify different user roles to allow the different access requirements to be highlighted in the design.

6.1.3 Interrelationships to other SSADM techniques/products

The following other areas of SSADM are related to Work Practice Modelling:

- **Business Activity Modelling**. The Work Practice Model is a mapping of the Business Activity Model onto an Organisation to specify who (which user roles) carries out each business activity and where the activities are carried out.

- **Data Flow Modelling**, in that the Current Physical Data Flow Model can be used as a source of information about current tasks that could be used as an input to Task Modelling.

- **Function Definition**, where Functions can be derived from Required Task Models. Functions are the IT facilities which require to be controlled to provide direct support to tasks.

- **Requirements Definition**, in that some of the results of User Analysis are documented in the Requirements Catalogue as usability requirements and the development of the Work Practice Model, Required Task Models and Task Scenarios will generate functional requirements.

- **User Object Modelling**, in that the User Object Model is derived with direct reference to the Required Task Models.

6.2   User Object Modelling

User Object Modelling allows the analyst to identify, analyse and develop a model of what the user will think is 'in the system' and how it is structured and organised. The User Object Model identifies the information which should be presented at the user interface, what associations are important to users, and the rules and relationships that should be preserved at the user interface. The user objects are what the user believes he/she is seeing and interacting with in the user interface. It is needed to develop an effective organisation of the user interface which makes it easy for the users to learn and control the system.

The value of performing User Object Modelling is that it:

- focuses the designer's attention on how users will understand and hence use the system;

- supports the designer in achieving an appropriate match between the system and user tasks;

- provides a clear structured description of the system and its user interface;

- provides a framework for detailed design;

- forms a stable baseline against which design alternatives can be assessed.

In addition the content of the user interface can be derived directly from the User Object Model.

6.2.1 Concepts of User Object Modelling

The main concepts for User Object Modelling are:

- **Action**, which is something the users performs in relation to the user interface of the computer system. It is through actions that the events and enquiries are invoked. All events and enquiries that are user initiated will be cross-referenced to actions.

- **Association**, which is a relationship between two user objects that the system will need to provide or enforce.

- **User Object**, which is something the user will want to recognise as a component of the user interface of the automated system. A user object may represent a set of data that the user wishes to view and/or change, a computer system user object or device with which the user will need to interact or a container of other user objects or data User objects are related to one another via associations, they have User Object Model (UOM) attributes and they have actions associated with them.

- **User Object Model (UOM) attributes**, which is an element of a user object as defined by the user within the context of their tasks some of which will have equivalents in the Logical Data Model.

6.2.2 Products of User Object Modelling

The main product of User Object Modelling is the User Object Model. A User Object Model is, in essence, a user's mental model of the structure and contents of the system. It identifies simple mapping rules that will allow the user to predict how the system operates.

It is made up of two parts:

- User Object Structure;

- User Object Description.

User Object Structure

A User Object Structure is a pictorial representation of the user objects, together with their UOM attributes, actions and interrelationships. It is similar to (but not the same as) a Logical Data Model, but in this case it is modelling the user's view of the objects within the system.

On the diagram:

- User Objects are represented by the boxes which contains details of UOM attributes and the actions for the user object;

- an association is represented by a line that joins two user object boxes.

An example of a User Object Structure is shown in Figure 6-3

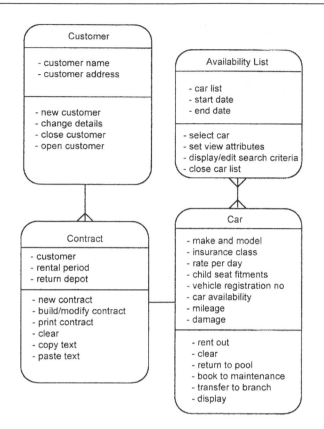

Figure 6-3 Example User Object Structure

User Object Description

For each user object in the User Object Structure there is an associated User Object Description which gives details for the user objects.

6.2.3 Interrelationships to other SSADM techniques/products

The following other areas of SSADM are related to User Object Modelling:

- **Work Practice Modelling**. The User Object Model is derived initially with reference to the information required to support tasks performed by all user roles. Where groups of user roles are interested in completely different sets of key objects, there may be a need to develop several User Object Models.

- **Logical Data Modelling**, in that the entities on the Logical Data Model can be cross-related to User Objects.

- **User Interface Design**, where the User Object Model is a primary input to User Interface Design. The user objects and their associations are supported by windows and window navigation. Window actions are an implementation of user object actions.

6.3   Function Definition

Function Definition identifies units of processing specification, or functions, which need to be controlled as a whole in order to support the users' tasks.

During the development project two types of function are identified:

- **On-line functions**, where the user interfaces directly with the system either to update some of the information stored within the system or to retrieve information stored by the system or, more normally, a combination of the two:

- **Off-line functions**, where the system operates without user intervention (e.g., back-up). This type of function is sometimes known as a Batch function.

This section deals solely with on-line functions. Off-line functions are described as part of Function Modelling which is covered in Chapter 5.

Functions can contain elements which are either on-line or off-line (Batch). The function elements which are on-line require a user interface and are therefore defined in a different way from function elements which operate without a user interface.

6.3.1 Concepts for Function Definition

The main concept for Function Definition is the function which can be defined as a unit of processing which is required to be controlled as a whole in support of a single task. Where the task requires several units of processing which do not directly interact, and do not need to be controlled together, there will be more than one function defined for that task.

There are three levels that need to be defined in order to be able to implement the processing required by an on-line function:

- **the presentation level** is the presentation of the function to the user. The same presentation may be used for more than one function. In some systems, it is possible to switch views at this level without changing the core objects or actions available to the user. An example of this would be the switching between 'Normal' and 'Page Layout' views in a word processing package;

- **the user interaction level** is where the user executes actions on user objects. There will be a number of actions that only operate at this level and others that will progress to the next level (conceptual model level). Examples of actions that remain at this level would be zooming, printing or keying in information before a 'save' action invokes an event;

- **the conceptual model level** is where an action invoked in the interface level is recognised as invoking an event or enquiry that requires access to the underlying persistent data as represented in the Logical Data Model. The action is interpreted into the appropriate event or enquiry trigger which is applied to the Logical Data Model in the way specified in Entity Behaviour Modelling (see the *Behaviour and Process Modelling* volume in this series). This level is specified by the cross-references between the User Object Model and events and enquiries.

6.3.2 Products for Function Definition

The main product of the Function Definition technique is the Function Description which consists of two parts:

- Function Description;

- Function Navigation Model.

Function Description

A Function Description contains some descriptive text and a large number of cross-references to other products.

Function Navigation Model

For very complex functions it may be useful to construct a diagram that shows how the different parts of the function relate to each other. This can be done either informally by walking through the different parts of the function or formally by the construction of a Function Navigation Model.

This model can be used to aid the analyst in understanding the function, help validate the function with the users or as an input to the construction of the Window Navigation Model.

It is not expected that this model will be produced for most functions, rather being only produced for very complex ones.

6.3.3 Interrelationships to other SSADM techniques/products

The following other areas of SSADM are related to Function Definition:

- **Logical Data Modelling**, where enquiry functions will validate that the Required System Logical Data Model can support the enquiry requirements. This may result in changes to the Logical Data Model being necessary.

- **Work Practice Modelling**, in that the tasks derived as part of Task Modelling will be used as the main input to the identification of on-line functions. Required Task Models are examined to identify whether a function is for the whole task or for sub-tasks requiring a user interface. Task Scenarios may help in the validation of functions.

- **Entity Behaviour Modelling**. All events and enquiries will be invoked via functions (this relationship is indirect where a User Object Model exists – in this case actions from the User Object Model invoke events and enquiries – functions then cross-reference the actions). The identification of functions often identifies the need for events and enquiries. Conversely, the examination of events and enquiries may help to determine what functions are required.

- **User Interface Design**, where functions are cross-referenced to the user objects and their actions. This cross-reference will be used as an input to the identification of views required for User Interface Design.

- **Requirements Definition**, in that the Requirements Catalogue contains details of the enquiries for the new system which will be defined as functions.

6.4   User Interface Design

User Interface Design is a representation of the interface in terms of windows and navigation through the system. The approach used within SSADM is of particular applicability to user interfaces which will be implemented using a Graphical User Interface (GUI).

The user interface is a vital part of the design of an automated system. For many systems, the user interface will be a complex area to design as it must fit in with the tasks of the user and be relatively straightforward to use. User Interface Design ensures that user roles from the User Organisation are given access to the elements of the stored data in a controlled and usable way. User Interface Design concentrates on the user's direct interaction with the system and is therefore of utmost importance in the analysis and design of a usable system.

The content of the user interface is mainly derived from the User Object Model although a number of other sources are used. What the user sees in windows is views of user objects upon which they will want to perform actions. The combination of windows and the constraints to be applied are dictated by the functions which in turn are based upon the definition of the users' tasks in the Required Task Models. The Installation Style Guide and Application Style Guide form the mechanism used to ensure that the installation and application standards are applied to screen and report layouts.

The relationships between the User Interface Design and other development project products is shown in Figure 6-4.

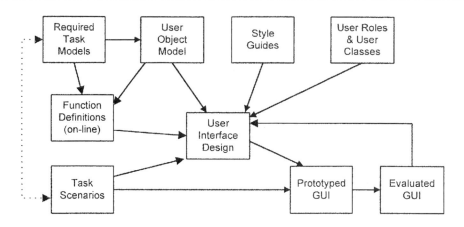

Figure 6-4 Relationship between User Interface Design products and other products

6.4.1 Concepts for User Interface Design

The following are the main concepts for User Interface Design:

- **Action**. An action is something the user performs in relation to the user interface of the computer system. Actions can appear as elements of sub-tasks in Task Models, as properties of user objects – an action is a definition of what can be done by a user to interact with a user object or as part of GUI Design where an action can be performed on controls within windows in the user interface.

- **Window**. A window is effectively a communication channel through which the user looks to view and interact with user objects from the User Object Model. Ideally, the context of the window should not affect the basic features and behaviour (UOM attributes and actions) of the user objects to which it is providing access. However, different views of the same object, seen in different windows, may contain different subsets of UOM attributes and allow different subsets of actions to be performed.

- **Control**. A control is an element of the user interface used to control the display, edit some value or start a command. Examples of user interface controls are a button, a scroll bar or a drop-down list. Controls need to be carefully selected to support the users' tasks.

- **State**. A user interface can be in a state or mode. This is where a set of commands has a particular meaning based on the previous commands. So a word processor could be in a page preview state where only some of the commands work the same way as in normal editing.

- **Style Guide**. Style Guides are of great importance in projects to ensure a common look and feel across all facilities within the application. This can offer benefits to users who will become familiar with new applications more rapidly if the interface works in the same way in all contexts. If the same style guide is adopted across all applications, the training required in the use of new applications will be greatly reduced for those users already familiar with existing applications. There are two main types of style guide:

- the Installation Style Guide which sets broad standards for all applications within the organisation as a whole;

- the Application Style Guide which is an elaboration of the Installation Style Guide for use on a particular project.

6.4.2 Products of User Interface Design

There are three products from User Interface Design. These are:

- Window Specifications;

- Window Navigation Model;

- Help System Specifications.

Window Specifications

A Window Specification is a detailed description of a window that will be used as the basis for the implementation of the window. Window Specifications can be developed at different levels of detail. For simple windows it is usually adequate to develop a rough hand-drawn sketch. For more complex, critical windows it is advised that the full specification detailed below is completed.

Window Navigation Model

The Window Navigation Model documents the relationships between windows. These relationships are driven by the needs of functions which support tasks. For complex functions it can be derived from the Function Navigation Models developed in Function Definition. A single Window Navigation Model is developed for the system as a whole based on individual functions. The constraints and controls required for specific functions will be built into the design and implementation of the final system.

The aim of developing the Window Navigation Model is to:

- ensure that the window structure supports the user tasks;

- check that window navigation is minimised and users don't have to switch between different dialog boxes to get the information they need;

- ensure task completion points match up with the overall window structure;

- identify common dialogue structures and handle them in a consistent way;

- ensure functionality is placed where it is needed;

- ensure that exit points are provided for all transactions so users can cancel a transaction or put it on hold.

The Window Navigation Model should be developed to cover all main windows and dialog boxes. It should not include every message or help window. Any general-purpose navigation should be included in the Application Style Guide. The Window Navigation Model for a system can become very complex and difficult to maintain so it should be developed with care. The aim is to check that the system will 'hang together', that navigation is minimised and to look for overlaps and common areas of dialogue.

Help System Specification

The Help System Specification should include the following:

- procedures that should be described in the help system;

- concepts that should be explained in the help system;

- field and dialog help (field-level help may be included in the Data Catalogue).

Help should be defined for the different audiences of the system and should be developed by technical writers with experience in help system development. There are two different types of help, un-requested help, such as messages that indicate what a function will do in a status bar, and user requested help.

6.4.3 Interrelationships to other SSADM techniques/products

The following other areas of SSADM are related to User Interface Design:

- **User Object Modelling**. User objects are the elements of the user interface with which the user interacts. The User Object Model is therefore a very important input to User Interface Design. Windows are based on user objects and the navigation between windows must support the associations between user objects.

- **Function Definition**. Functions are the automated facilities provided by the IT application to support the users' tasks. Functions therefore provide the bridge between Task Modelling and User Interface Design. Function Navigation Models provide the basis for the Window Navigation Model.

- **Prototyping and Evaluation**, which are a necessary part of User Interface Design. The initial windows and navigation designed using the techniques and products described in this chapter need to be brought to life and demonstrated to users to ensure that they meet their requirements.

- **Work Practice Modelling**, in that the User Interface Design must support the tasks of the user. This means that the whole of User Interface Design is influenced by the products of Work Practice Modelling.

6.5   Prototyping and Evaluation

A prototype is a model or example used to help envisage the finished article during the design process. Prototyping can take a number of different forms and can be used for several different purposes. Some types of prototype are treated as initial versions of the system which are iteratively refined into the delivered system. Other types of prototype are used for a particular purpose and then thrown away. With the increasing use of Graphical User Interfaces (GUIs), prototyping is becoming more of an integral part of any project.

GUI prototyping is concerned with developing a working example of the user interface that users can interact with. It is iterative and involves the user in evaluating the user interface. It is this type of prototyping that is covered in SSADM.

Evaluation involves the setting of the prototyping scope and assessing the results of the prototype. It is an important part of the overall prototyping process as it establishes what changes are required to the user interface as a result of prototyping. The objectives of evaluation are to identify usability problems, to assess whether the GUI design satisfies specified usability requirements and to evaluate whether the GUI design will be usable in practice by its intended users.

Prototyping the user interface and evaluating it with users is a vital part of the process. Early prototyping can help save costly mistakes by clarifying assumptions and validating requirements. However, care is needed when developing early user interface prototypes to manage users' expectations on development timescales and functionality.

6.5.1 Concepts of Prototyping and Evaluation

There are three important concepts when looking at prototypes:

- **Scope**. The scope of a prototype defines how much or how little of the user interface design is prototyped. A prototype can vary between having a narrow scope and having a wide scope. A prototype with a narrow scope may focus on a complex window which is causing users problems. A prototype with wide scope may look at navigation around the whole system.

- **Fidelity**. The fidelity of a prototype is the degree to which the prototype is detailed or realistic. A prototype can vary between being of low fidelity and being of high fidelity. A low fidelity prototype may be hand-drawn sketches used to validate requirements. A high fidelity prototype would use the correct colours, fonts and would position all items with the right separation in a window.

- **Functionality**. The functionality of a prototype is the degree to which the data appearing on the screen and functionality is 'working' or 'live' or how much is simulated. Simulated functionality can be used to test design concepts and working functionality may be used to test the usability of the system and to allow users more choice when using a prototype.

6.5.2 Products of Prototyping and Evaluation

There are three products for Prototyping and Evaluation. These are:

- objectives for the prototype;
- results of the prototype;
- the prototype itself.

Objectives for the prototype

A prototype needs clearly defined objectives and scope. The objectives are set by
determining what you want to learn or achieve with the prototype. It is important to
understand the objectives and scope before prototyping is commenced as this will help in
the management of prototyping and limit the number of iterations. Far too many prototypes
fail to achieve anything because the analysts and the users have never agreed a common
agenda for the prototyping exercise.

Results of the prototype

The results of the evaluation can be analysed in a number of different ways. The detailed
notes kept during prototyping sessions can be written up into a brief report which
summarises:

- good and bad points of the design;
- comments made by users;
- print-out of the user interface with problem areas marked,
- prioritised list of problems;
- any performance or error metrics.

Once the evaluation has been concluded changes to the design need to be agreed and
documented and these can feed into the next prototype or provide input to the
Requirements Specification. The aim must be to identify improvements that have direct
business benefit by improving the usability of the system.

The prototype itself

There is often an underlying assumption that prototypes should aim to be presented on
screens to users, preferably with a wide scope, reasonable fidelity and enough functionality
to 'convince' a user that this could be real. However, this approach has two main
disadvantages:

- this type of prototype can be relatively costly to develop and takes a significant
  amount of time;
- the closer the prototype looks to the 'real thing' the more difficult it is to keep the
  user's expectations realistic and to make the user concentrate on the issues being
  addressed by the prototype.

Consideration should be given to using more 'low-tech' prototypes which can, with some
effort, achieve the same results as automated prototypes but quicker, cheaper and with
fewer problems with user expectations. The analyst can use paper prototypes or story
boards to 'walk through' an area of the design. These are low fidelity prototypes with
simulated data and functionality.

6.5.3 Interrelationships to other SSADM techniques/products

The following other areas of SSADM are related to Prototyping and Evaluation:

- **User Interface Design**. User Interface Design and prototyping are closely connected with one another. The user interface can be designed initially using User Interface Design techniques but it needs to be prototyped and evaluated before it can be considered stable. Thus, the user interface should be developed iteratively or in parallel using design and prototyping to build on one another.

- **Work Practice Modelling**, which provides the definition of users' tasks which are to be supported by dialogues. The scope of individual prototypes would normally be based upon Task Scenarios.

- **Requirements Definition**. New requirements may be uncovered by prototyping and evaluation or requirements may need to be modified.

7   BEHAVIOUR AND PROCESS MODELLING[5]

Within SSADM Behaviour and Process Modelling is concerned with the construction of models which show the system's view of the requirements. These models can be divided into two categories:

- **Entity Behaviour Models**, which identifies the triggers (events and enquiries) that will cause the system to update its stored data and then shows how these triggers effect the stored data over time. This involves the development of the Entity Access Matrix, the Event and Enquiry Catalogue and the Entity Life Histories.

- **Conceptual Process Models**, which define the processing requirements for the system which result from the event and enquiry triggers. This involves the development of Enquiry Access Paths, Effect Correspondence Diagrams, Enquiry Process Models and Update Process Models.

These two areas are very powerful in that they turn the analysis models that have already been produced (e.g., Requirements Catalogue and Logical Data Models) into the processing requirements that will need to be developed for the new system.

Within Behaviour and Process Modelling the models that are developed are generally independent of the physical architecture for the new system. This gives a number of advantages, among them:

- the models are developed to a common standard thus aiding with readability;

- the architecture of the new system does not need to be fully defined at the time the models are developed;

- the designers developing the models do not need a deep understanding of the physical architecture of the new system.

7.1   Entity Behaviour Modelling

Entity Behaviour Modelling covers a set of techniques which model the interaction between data and processes. Three areas are covered:

- Event Identification;

- Enquiry Identification;

- Entity Life Histories.

Event Identification is a technique which identifies all events by examination of the Required System Data Flow Model and Required System Logical Data Model.

---

[5] This chapter contains an overview of the concepts, products and techniques for behaviour and process modelling. For a full description of all the concepts, products, techniques and interrelationships for behaviour and process modelling, see the *Behaviour and Process Modelling* volume in this series.

Enquiry Identification is a technique which identifies enquiries by examining the information support requirements for business activities and from user requirements. Enquiries are used to help build and validate the Logical Data Model (see the *Data Modelling* volume in this series).

The Entity Life History Analysis technique which is regarded as a major analysis and design technique is used to model the sequence of events which affect specific entities on the Required System Logical Data Model. This is done in order to define constraints on the updating of entities and to explore the required degree to which business events and business rules are reflected in requirements for updating of data within the system. The results of Entity Life History Analysis are fed into Conceptual Process Modelling.

7.1.1 Concepts of Entity Behaviour Modelling

The following are the main concepts for Entity Behaviour Modelling:

- **Event**. An event is something that triggers a process to update the system data. It is usually sourced by a business event, notified to the system via one or more functions. An event provides the reason for an update process to be initiated. The name of the event should be a noun clause and should reflect what is causing the process to be invoked – not the process name itself. Typical event names might include terms such as 'Receipt', 'Notification', 'Decision', 'Arrival', 'New', 'Change'.

- **Enquiry**. An enquiry is something that triggers a process to extract information from the system data without updating the data in any way.

- **Entity Life History** An Entity Life History (ELH) charts all of the events that may cause a particular entity occurrence to change in some way and places them in sequence. An Entity Life History is a structured diagram showing a combination of all possible lives for every occurrence of an entity. Each occurrence is constrained to act in the way defined by the Entity Life History for that entity.

- **Effect**. The change within a single entity occurrence caused by an event is called an effect. Each effect is documented on the Entity Life History diagram for the relevant entity.

- **Effect Qualifiers**. An occurrence of an entity may be affected in one of several mutually exclusive ways by an event. A single occurrence of an event will result in only one type of effect. Each possible effect is separately identified on the Entity Life History diagram by using the event name qualified by a description of the effect enclosed in round brackets.

- **Entity Role**. If a single occurrence of an event affects more than one occurrence of a particular entity and the effects are different, the entity has a different role for each different type of effect. Entity roles are identified by adding them to effect boxes on the Entity Life History enclosed in square brackets. An effect can have both an entity role and an effect qualifier but is more likely to have either one or the other.

7.1.2 Products of Entity Behaviour Modelling

The products of Entity Behaviour Modelling are as follows:

- Entity Access Matrix;

- Event and Enquiry Catalogue;

- Entity Life Histories.

Entity Access Matrix

The Entity Access Matrix is a powerful working document that helps to identify which entities are affected or accessed by a particular event or enquiry. Entities (including entity aspects and sub-super-types) from the Required System Logical Data Model are placed along one axis of the matrix and events and enquiries are placed along the other axis as they are discovered. Intersections of the matrix are completed to indicate the type of access. If an event accesses an entity in several different ways (possibly in different contexts) several entries can be made in a single intersection of the matrix.

Event and Enquiry Catalogue

The Event and Enquiry Catalogue records information about the important characteristics of each event and enquiry. This is likely to be in the form of a report from a CASE tool.

Entity Life Histories

An Entity Life History (ELH) is a diagram which charts the life of an entity from birth to death within a system in terms of the events which affect it. An Entity Life History is a model of what can happen to entity occurrences over time, and is read from left to right in chronological order of events.

Entity Life Histories use a notation with sequences, selections, iterations and parallel structures as the basic structure components. Operations can be added to the bottom boxes of the structure (effects) and state indicators are added below these to indicate the status of the entity at any point in its life.

Each effect (bottom leaf of the structure) contains the name of an event. Where the same event appears more than once within the structure, the event name is qualified by an effect qualifier, enclosed in round brackets, and/or entity role, enclosed in square brackets.

The top box of the structure contains the name of the entity for which this diagram is drawn. Entity Life Histories contain the following components:

- **sequence** represented by a box with a series of plain boxes below it: the plain boxes should be read from left to right;

- **iteration** represented by a box with a single box below it containing an asterisk in the top right corner: the lower box can be repeated a number of times from zero to many;

- **selection** represented by a box with a series of boxes below it each of which contains an 'o' in the top right corner: these boxes are alternatives for one another, only one of which will be selected at this point in the structure (if one of boxes is a 'null' selection, indicated by a dash, then it is possible for none of the alternatives to be selected);

- **parallel structure** represented by a parallel bar above two or more boxes: each leg of the parallel structure is visited but in no particular sequence.

In addition two optional components can be added to the diagram:

- **state indicators,** which can be thought of as an additional attribute within each entity which can be used to ascertain where, in the entity's life history this occurrence is

- **operations**, which are discrete units of logical processing which, either singularly or in combination with others, constitutes an event's effect.

An example of a basic ELH (without state indicator and operations) is shown in Figure 7-1.

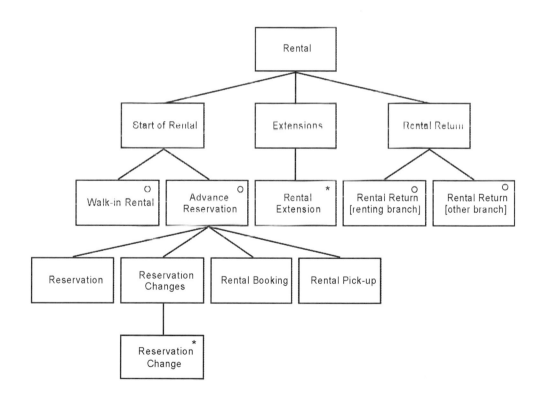

Figure 7-1 Example Entity Life History

7.1.3 Interrelationships to other SSADM techniques/products

The following other areas of SSADM are related to Entity Behaviour Modelling:

- **Business Activity Modelling**, in that the Business Activity Model contains a definition of business events. From these definitions, the set of events that will used in Entity Behaviour Modelling can be derived.

- **Function Definition**. Function Definition helps to identify events and enquiries and group them within functions. An event/enquiry may be input via more than one function and so be referenced by several Function Descriptions. For each function the analyst must check to see that the attributes for the event/enquiry are contained in the input to or can be generated by the function.

- **Logical Data Modelling**. The Required System Logical Data Model contains the entities upon which Entity Life Histories are based and is used to create the Entity Access Matrix in the first instance. The detailed data analysis in the Entity Life History technique is likely to improve the practitioner's understanding of the entities in the system and may lead to substantial changes being made to the Logical Data Model. In addition, the definition of enquiries are a powerful tool in the development and validation of the Logical Data Model.

- **Conceptual Process Modelling,** where the Conceptual Process Modelling products are derived directly from Entity Behaviour Modelling products. Effect Correspondence Diagrams are derived from the Entity Life Histories and Entity Access Matrix. Enquiry Access Paths are drawn for each of the enquiries identified.

7.2   Conceptual Process Modelling

Conceptual Process Modelling defines the processing required in response to events or enquiries. Conceptual Process Modelling covers a set of techniques which model the accessing of the Required System Logical Data Model by events and enquiries and the operations required to support the processing of the events and enquiries.

There are four techniques for Conceptual Process Modelling;

- **Enquiry Access Paths,** which validates the Required System Logical Data Model by testing it against requirements for information support to the business, specifies enquiries in an unambiguous way and creates structures for enquiry processes;

- **Effect Correspondence Diagrams,** which provides similar structures for update processes;

- **Enquiry Process Models,** which transform Enquiry Access Paths into structures which present the enquiry processes in a format that will provide a route through into physical design for certain types of environment (e.g., 3GL with tight performance constraints);

- **Update Process Models** which transform Effect Correspondence Diagrams into structures which present the update processes in a format that will provide a route through into physical design for certain types of environment (e.g., 3GL with tight performance constraints).

7.2.1 Products for Conceptual Process Modelling

Within Conceptual Process Modelling, there are four basic products:

- Enquiry Access Paths;
- Effect Correspondence Diagrams;
- Enquiry Process Models;
- Update Process Models.

Effect Correspondence Diagrams and Enquiry Access Paths are similar in structure and so are dealt with together below. Likewise a similar approach is taken to the description of Enquiry Process Models and Update Process Models.

Effect Correspondence Diagrams and Enquiry Access Paths

An Effect Correspondence Diagram (ECD) shows the way in which effects for each event are related to one another and demonstrates the navigation around the Required System Logical Data Model required to process the effects. Similarly, Enquiry Access Paths show all the accesses required of entities on the Logical Data Model and the navigation paths required to retrieve the specified data.

For both types of diagram, the entry point into the Logical Data Model is indicated by an arrow annotated with the data items that are provided with the event or enquiry in order to identify the correct entity occurrences and to supply values for attributes required for the event or enquiry processes to be completed. Navigation is indicated by a series of arrows between boxes. Each box represents an effect/access or is a node used to indicate selection or iteration.

The overall title of the diagram contains the enquiry or event name. The basic structure contains the following components:

- selection represented by a box with two or more boxes below it, each of which contains an 'o' in the top right corner;
- iteration represented by a box with a single box below it containing an asterisk '*' in the top right corner;
- one-to-one navigation arrows between two boxes of any type except the following:
  - between two iterated components (indicated by an asterisk);
  - between two selected components (indicated by an 'o');
  - between a selected component and an iterated component.

An example Enquiry Access Path is shown in Figure 7-2.

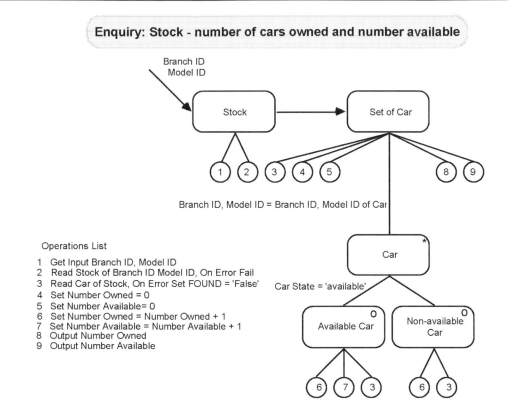

Figure 7-2 An example Enquiry Access Path

Update Process Models and Enquiry Process Models

Enquiry and Update Process Models are a transformation of Enquiry Access Paths and Effect Correspondence Diagrams into structures.

All boxes on the diagram are 'hard' boxes. The top box of the structure contains the name of the event or enquiry. The structure contains the following components:

- **sequence** represented by a box with a series of plain boxes below it: the plain boxes should be read from left to right;

- **iteration** represented by a box with a single box below it containing an asterisk in the top right corner: the process represented by this box can be repeated a number of times from zero to many;

- **selection** represented by a box with a series of boxes below it containing 'o' in the top right corner: these boxes are alternatives for one another, only one of which will be selected at this point in the structure (if one of the boxes is a 'null' selection, indicated by a dash, then it is possible for none of the alternatives to be selected);

Each bottom leaf on the structure represents the processing of an effect or access from the Effect Correspondence Diagram or Enquiry Access Path. Some more operations can be added to the boxes on the structure in the sequence in which they are invoked. Operations can be added to structure boxes as well as the 'leaves' of the structure.

An example of an Update Process Model is shown in Figure 7-3.

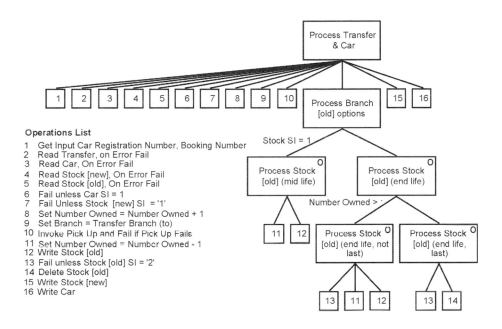

Operations List

1 Get Input Car Registration Number, Booking Number
2 Read Transfer, on Error Fail
3 Read Car, On Error Fail
4 Read Stock [new], On Error Fail
5 Read Stock [old], On Error Fail
6 Fail unless Car SI = 1
7 Fail Unless Stock [new] SI = '1'
8 Set Number Owned = Number Owned + 1
9 Set Branch = Transfer Branch (to)
10 Invoke Pick Up and Fail if Pick Up Fails
11 Set Number Owned = Number Owned - 1
12 Write Stock [old]
13 Fail unless Stock [old] SI = '2'
14 Delete Stock [old]
15 Write Stock [new]
16 Write Car

Figure 7-3 Example Update Process Model

7.2.2 Interrelationships to other SSADM techniques/products

The following other areas of SSADM are related to Conceptual Process Modelling:

- **Entity Behaviour Modelling**, which identifies events and enquiries and considers their interaction with entities. The interaction between events and entities is modelled using Entity Life Histories. Conceptual Process Modelling takes the products of Entity Behaviour Modelling and uses them directly to produce Enquiry Access Paths and Effect Correspondence Diagrams.

- **Logical Data Modelling**, in that the Logical Data Structure is used to determine the correspondences between effects in Effect Correspondence Diagrams and Enquiry Access Paths. It is also used to check the data items used as event/enquiry data.

- **Physical Process Design**, where the Conceptual Process Modelling products are developed into physical specifications during Physical Process Design.

8   DATABASE AND PHYSICAL PROCESS DESIGN[6]

The purpose of Database and Physical Process Design is to specify the physical data and processes for the new system using the language and features of the chosen physical environment and incorporating installation standards. The integrity of the Logical Design is maintained as far as possible, whilst exploiting the strengths of the implementation products and minimising their weaknesses. Essential performance requirements are also addressed.

Database and Physical Process Design consists of two activities:

- **Database Design**, in which the Logical Data Model for the new system is turned into a physical design which is architecturally correct. Often this task actually involves the building of the database itself.

- **Physical Process Design**, in which the products of the Logical Design which contain elements of processing (e.g., functions) are used to produce a environment specific process specifications. These are often known as Program Specifications.

Following Database and Physical Process Design, no further specification or design activity should be necessary to enable the system to be developed. Indeed, it is probable that a significant proportion of components will have already been constructed.

The products of Database and Physical Process Design are a mapping of the logical design products developed earlier in the project onto the physical environment, in accordance with any installation standards. This mapping will rarely be a direct translation of the logical design products onto their physical equivalents. Instead, it will usually be necessary to change some elements of them in order to take advantage of features of the technology and to ensure that performance objectives are met. Optimising the Database and Physical Process Design will require trade-offs between factors such as space, performance, ease of use, portability and maintainability. Any change should be as the result of conscious decisions and should be documented.

Database and Physical Process Design should not in itself alter the Logical Design. However, if, during Database and Physical Process Design, flaws in the Logical Design are revealed, the designers should revise the Logical Design and work forward from there. It is important to retain a logical specification distinct from its mapping onto a specific technology as this can be used during maintenance of the system and can be a useful starting point if the need arises to implement the same system on a different platform.

---

[6] This chapter contains an overview of the concepts, products and techniques for database and physical process design. For a full description of all the concepts, products, techniques and interrelationships for database and physical process design, see the *Database and Physical Process Design* volume in this series.

8.1   Database Design

Database Design is concerned with the physical placement of data and the impact that this placement has on access to the data. Database Design is a complex subject and is not covered comprehensively within SSADM. Additional skills and knowledge about the technical environment and the data management software are needed.

The objective of Database Design is to develop a design which:

- implements the new system's data requirements, as defined in the Required System Logical Data Model;

- supports the system's processing requirements;

- meets the space and timing objectives set for the system.

In developing a Database Design the following must be addressed:

- to produce an efficient Database Design from a Logical Data Model, the designer must have a thorough understanding of the chosen implementation environment;

- the designer needs to know how far to optimise the design. The aim is to produce a design that is good enough to meet the system performance objectives;

- system performance objectives may conflict with other requirements, for example ,maintainability, development time, storage constraints;

To tackle these problems the Database Design technique provides a general framework for the design team to follow. This can be tailored as necessary. If the design team follows the this framework the database designer is required to perform the following activities:

- define a strategy to be followed in Database Design;

- produce a Database Design;

- test and optimise the Database Design where necessary, to meet the performance objectives.

In order to do this, the database designer may need to first gain an understanding of the implementation environment and identify facilities and constraints within the implementation environment which will have an impact on the production of the physical specification.

8.2   Products for Database Design

The main product of Database Design is the Database Design.

In addition, during the conduct of Database Design a number of intermediate products may be produced to assist the database designer. These intermediate products may be provided from outside the project or may be developed specifically for the project and may include:

- Physical Design Strategy;

- DBMS classifications;

- Space and Timing estimation spreadsheets.

Database Design

The scope of the term Database Design is very broad. In SSADM, the term refers specifically to the study of the complex issues of:

- physical data placement;

- DBMS optimisation.

SSADM provides general rules of thumb applicable to most DBMSs or file handlers for quickly producing an initial physical data model. Product-specific rules can then be applied. Timing and sizing is carried out on the design and, if necessary, changes are made to the design to meet performance and space objectives.

The form of the Database Design will be directly related to the environment in which it is to implemented.

An example of a completed SSADM Database Design is shown in Figure 9-1

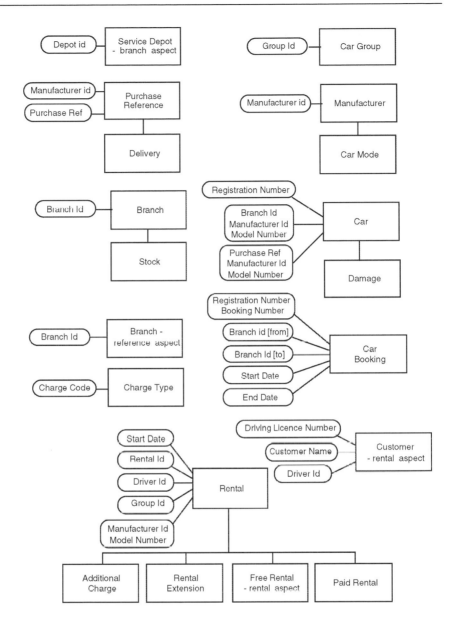

Figure 8-1 Example of Database Design

Physical Design Strategy

In organisations where a new Database Management System (DBMS) is being introduced or this is the first project to implement a database on the DBMS, it may be useful to develop a strategy for Database Design. In many cases, the method for Database Design will be well established within the organisation.

DBMS classifications

From descriptions of the database facilities and features, it may be useful to develop a classification of data storage characteristics and performance.

Space and Timing estimation spreadsheets

These can be used to check whether the Database Design is likely to meet space and timing objectives. They can be used during optimisation of the design.

8.2.1 Interrelationships to other SSADM techniques/products

The following other areas of SSADM are related to Database Design:

- **Logical Data Modelling**. The Required System Logical Data Model is the major input to Database Design. It is necessary to ensure that all volumes and entry points are documented on the Logical Data Model.

- **Requirements Definition** in that all non-functional requirements are potentially useful in the optimisation of the Database Design.

- **Function Definition**. Optimisation is directed towards the performance of critical functions. The functions define the grouping of invocations of the event and enquiry processes (specified in Conceptual Process Modelling) which will be used for the detail of performance estimates. Service level requirements for critical functions will be useful as an input to optimisation. Also, volumes of critical functions will be required.

- **Technical System Options**, in that the Technical System Architecture may give useful information to the designers.

8.3   Physical Process Design

Physical Process Design deals with the conversion of the products of logical design into physical program specifications for the chosen physical environment. The technique guides designers in the approach to specifying a system's physical processes, from Logical Design, taking into account information about the selected physical processing system they are working with.

Physical Process Design covers a defined but generic range of design aspects and to a limited depth.

It should be noted that within SSADM this technique deals solely with the definition of Physical Process Designs. Screen, Interface and Window design is covered by the User Centred Design.

There is interaction with a number of other areas of SSADM. The Requirements Catalogue provides much of the information about what is needed in the new system. The Technical System Architecture, developed within the Decision Structure, provides the basic technical architecture for the new system. User procedures within the organisation will act as constraints on what is developed or will be devised as part of Physical Process Design.

Another major input to Physical Process Design will come from within the Policies and Procedures of the organisation. These will provide the following:

- **Processing System Classification**. This will identify the features of the implementation technology that can be used. The precise features will depend upon the technology chosen but may include the types of tools that are available, mix of procedural and non-procedural languages, database processing and user interface interaction features;

- **Application Development Standards**. These standards will define criteria for deciding on the implementation technology for different components of functions, how to use the features of the implementation technology, how to undertake Physical Process Design and the standards for program specification. Many organisations will already have standards which can be used and adapted by specific projects. Where no standards exist, these will need to be developed before Physical Process Design is initiated.

8.3.1 *Products of Physical Process Design*

There may be many products developed as part of Physical Process Design depending upon local standards and policies. The following products are the ones defined within SSADM:

- Function Component Implementation Map;

- Process Data Interface;

- Program Specifications.

Function Component Implementation Map (FCIM)

The Function Component Implementation Map provides the overall structure of Physical Process Design. It defines:

- how logical specification components are grouped to define the content of physical components;

- how physical components fit together, including where components are reused.

The Function Component Implementation Map is supported by specifications for procedural fragments (the non-procedural fragments will generally be described using the language of the implementation environment itself).

The representation of the Function Component Implementation Map will vary from project to project, depending on the repository or dictionary facilities available. Possibilities include:

- if a single repository is used for logical and physical components, a set of logical-physical associations in the repository;

- if separate repositories are used for logical and physical components, a separate product maintaining logical-physical cross-references; for example, a diagram, a table, a small database.

Process Data Interface

The Process Data Interface is a layer of software that hides the physical database from the database update and enquiry processes in the conceptual model. The database processes can then be written as if for the Logical Data Model. At its simplest, the Process Data Interface might just be views of base tables and SQL calls to access them, embedded in database processes written in a host language such as COBOL or C.

Program Specifications

The designer may use non-procedural languages supplied with the physical environment to define the physical format of batch input and output data, and intermediate files. In some cases the analyst will also define database access paths in this way.

For some procedural elements of the system, the designer may need to use the principles of program design which underlie both the Structured Design Method (SDM) and Jackson Structured Programming (JSP). Alternatively for other procedural elements of the system or where a tool especially facilitates this approach, the designer may use a fragment or program specification.

8.3.2 Interrelationships to other SSADM techniques/products

The following other areas of SSADM are related to Physical Process Design:

- **Function Definition**. Function Definitions are a major input to Physical Process Design. Functions are part of External Design. For many functions, the mapping from the user interface to event/enquiry trigger is simple but for some there is a significant process, distinct from the window design, which is required to interpret user interface inputs into event/enquiry input and transform event/enquiry output into physical output. During the creation of the Function Component Implementation Map, syntactic errors, which will be detected by the input processes, are specified and common processes identified.

- **User Interface Design**. The products of User Interface Design (Window Navigation Model, Window Specifications and Help System Specifications) are examined to check that no gap exists between them and the Physical Process Designs and that any 'messaging' components are fully supplied.

- **Conceptual Process Modelling**. The Effect Correspondence Diagrams, Enquiry Access Paths, Update Processes Models and Enquiry Process Models will provide the basis for the definition of database processing within the system. Operations and conditions from Conceptual Process Modelling products can be directly implemented in a non-procedural language. In addition, new physical processes may be required which implement business rules that are not embedded in event and enquiry processes.

- **Database Design**. New performance requirements identified in Database Design will form part of the Process Data Interface. These may take the form of sort routines in batch run units. Such processes may be triggered and reported back by on-line processes.

9   PROJECT MANAGEMENT CONSIDERATIONS

This chapter gives details of project management considerations related to SSADM. It covers:

- take-on of SSADM;

- management of an SSADM project;

- the business case for SSADM;

- customisation of SSADM.

It should be noted that this chapter is not meant to replace the use of a standard project management method (e.g., PRINCE2) but rather to provide details that may be of use when using such a method to manage an SSADM project.

9.1   Getting started with SSADM

This section is aimed at individuals or organisations intending to adopt the Structured Systems Analysis and Design Method (SSADM) for the first time. It describes a recommended approach to introducing SSADM into an organisation, based on practical experience.

9.1.1 SSADM Infrastructure

SSADM was initially introduced as a standard for development projects undertaken within government departments. It was soon adopted by private sector organisations and is currently used as a de facto standard in a significant number of public and private sector organisations worldwide. The method was initially commissioned and funded by Central Computer and Telecommunications Agency (CCTA). Since its initial introduction in 1981, SSADM has remained under the overall control of CCTA which has provided the funding for its on-going development and enhancement.

The following may provide you with more information about SSADM:

- CCTA has developed a wide range of best practice guides which are designed to help with the development of information systems. Many of the guides cover aspects of using SSADM in practice in specific types of situation;

- the International SSADM Users Group has a wide membership consisting of public and private organisations and individuals. Meetings and conferences are organised where practical aspects of using SSADM are discussed and new areas are described. In addition, a newsletter is published which will give you all the latest news and views;

- there are many commercial organisations which supply training and consultancy services in SSADM. Their details can be found in the Directory of Services available from the International SSADM Users Group.

In addition, the Information Systems Examination Board (ISEB) are responsible for administering examinations and awarding diplomas and certificates in SSADM and related areas. ISEB exist as part of the British Computer Society (BCS).

9.1.2 Recommended approach for introducing SSADM into an Organisation

Obviously, each organisation will be different. The following factors will vary significantly from organisation to organisation:

- size – the problems of introducing SSADM into a large organisation are likely to be very different from those in a smaller organisation;

- responsibilities of different areas of the organisation – in some organisations, the provision of IT services will be a discrete part of the organisation, in others, responsibility will be diversified across several different areas and in others, it will be outsourced altogether;

- current culture – some organisations may already have other methods in place or be switching from another structured method to SSADM. In other organisations, staff will not be used to working in a structured way and the whole culture may have to change;

- skills – some organisations may already employ experienced analysts and designers and others may be setting up an IT function for the first time;

- geographical distribution – some organisations may be centralised in a single location, other organisations may have staff dispersed throughout several different locations.

With these potentially very wide variations, it would not be possible to provide a single approach. Some general principles are described below, but these will need to be considered in the context of your particular situation. An assumption is made in the remainder of this chapter that the organisation will be moderately large with more than 20 systems analysts and resources to set up training courses in-house. For smaller organisations, a more informal approach may be more appropriate which involves the use of public training courses.

Where much of the analysis and development work is outsourced, the organisation will need to gain awareness of SSADM in order to manage and control the outsourced organisation. In some cases, early stages will be undertaken by in-house analysts or users will be required to review SSADM products. Some training and awareness will be required and this should be carefully considered when adopting SSADM as a standard.

In summary, an approach for introducing SSADM into an organisation will probably need to cover the following:

- preparation;

- short-term actions;

- medium-term actions.

Preparation

In order to prepare for the take-on of SSADM, it is advised that some support is obtained from a supplier or individual with substantial practical experience in SSADM. This 'expert' support should undertake the following:

- investigate existing procedures, standards, methods, training in organisation;
- specify SSADM tailoring to fit into local project life cycles;
- define plan for SSADM implementation.

These are described further in the following paragraphs.

Investigation of Existing Practice

Existing procedures, standards, methods, training in the user organisation should be studied to determine:

- the existing level of knowledge and use of SSADM techniques among project staff, for example, some staff may have become familiar with SSADM or some of its techniques in previous employments and may be using areas of the method informally on projects;
- whether any SSADM techniques or similar methods are part of the existing training within the organisation;
- other parts of the organisation's project life cycle or development standards with which SSADM will have to interface; e.g., project definition, programming, quality assurance, hardware and software procurement, specialist roles (database administrator, procurement group);
- compatibility between SSADM and existing standards;
- awareness and attitudes of staff at all levels to the proposed introduction of SSADM.

Specify SSADM Tailoring

SSADM's structure and documentation may have to be modified to fit into the organisation's project life cycles and standards. This should be kept to a minimum as many of the advantages of taking on a standard structured method will be lost if tailoring is too extensive. The advantages that could be lost include:

- choice of supply of training and consultancy organisations;
- low cost, standard training with qualifications awarded by the Information Systems Examination Board (ISEB);
- off-the shelf reference material and books;
- substantial experience built up by a range of staff in other organisations who would require little extra training if recruited into this organisation;

- updates to the method and infrastructure supplied by CCTA.

The costs of developing a complete 'bespoke' version of SSADM are relatively high as this effectively becomes a new method. As a result, many organisations prefer to change their other procedures to fit in with SSADM, to minimise the overheads of taking on SSADM updates and extensions.

Tailoring of SSADM will require the development of reference material and training material.

Even where SSADM is not tailored, it will be necessary to produce guidelines on how SSADM can be used in conjunction with existing standards.

Define Plan for SSADM Implementation

The plan for implementing SSADM in an organisation should take into account the levels of awareness and acceptance of a new method and the current levels of skill within the organisation. It may be necessary to start with a series of overview presentations of SSADM, discussing how it will fit into the organisation, presented to audiences ranging from senior management to analysts and programmers. In any organisation, the success of implementing SSADM will rely very much on the degree of acceptance and commitment from all staff.

Plans may then include the following, depending upon the size of the organisation and the way in which it wishes to organise support for SSADM:

- training for in-house trainers and the joint running of training courses within the organisation between a commercial training organisation and the in-house team;
- identification of key people within the organisation who will form an SSADM support group. These people will need to gain experience of using SSADM on the earliest projects undertaken using SSADM so that they will subsequently be able to offer advice to other projects;
- identification of a pilot project to demonstrate the use of SSADM within the organisation;
- an on-going schedule of projects which should use SSADM.

It is assumed in this approach that a user organisation will want to become largely self-supporting in SSADM as soon as possible.

The first projects that adopt SSADM within the organisation are of critical importance to the success of SSADM. In most cases, a 'pilot' project should be identified which can be used to demonstrate the use of the method and train key staff. The objectives of a pilot project include the following:

- to confirm that SSADM will work in the organisation; the project must deliver acceptable working systems;
- to establish how the use of SSADM in the organisation might be improved in:

- following the method framework;

- use of individual techniques;

- documentation;

- planning, estimating and progress control;

- quality assurance;

- use of software support tools. Where a new software support/CASE tool is to be selected for the organisation as part of the introduction of SSADM, it is useful to make this selection prior to the pilot project and acquire at least one copy of the tool so that it can be 'tried out' in practice on the pilot project.

- to develop a nucleus of experienced staff who will form a centre of expertise in SSADM, and will in the future act as internal consultants and trainers.

The selection criteria for an ideal pilot project are:

- 9 – 12 months, from project brief to start of programming;

- mix of current activity and new development;

- significant requirements for both data design and process design;

- requiring a team of 3 – 5 staff;

- non-critical for delivery date.

It may not be possible to find projects with all of these characteristics. In many cases, SSADM has been piloted on very large or very small projects.

Short-term Actions

Once the plans have been developed by the 'expert' support, it is necessary for the organisation to start implementing them. The short-term actions that should be taken include the following:

- accept plans and tailored SSADM material;

- arrange and run awareness seminars;

- acquire software support tools;

- develop training plan;

- run initial training (practitioners and users);

- start pilot project;

- address requirement for training and support of team leaders and local experts.

Medium-term Actions

When the initial start-up tasks have been completed, some further actions need to be performed by the organisation:

- run pilot project and collect feedback;

- provide further training/support for team leaders and local experts;

- train internal trainers to present practitioner courses;

- review lessons learned on pilots and update method;

- initiate second wave of projects;

- integrate planning and estimating, QA with organisation's project management tools.

9.2   Managing SSADM Projects

SSADM alone cannot guarantee the success of a project. The method can only deliver its benefits when it is properly managed and controlled. SSADM addresses the analysis and design activities only, leaving the project management issues to other methods or approaches such as the PRINCE2 method. As it is not always easy to see how SSADM fits into a project management method/approach, this chapter aims to give some practical advice to project managers on the issues that must be addressed when SSADM is applied to a project. Although the concepts here are based very largely on the PRINCE2 method, they can be applied whatever the project management approach taken.

The areas of a project that must be considered which are not covered explicitly by SSADM include:

- Deciding on the approach to take;

- Project Initiation and Start-Up;

- Planning;

- Quality Management;

- Monitoring and Control.

These subject areas are expanded below.

9.2.1 *Deciding on the approach to take*

SSADM is a flexible method that can be used within a number of different life cycle approaches. It can be tailored towards a variety of different application environments and systems of varying sizes.

A particular issue that needs to be addressed by many managers is the need to deliver a quality system in as short a time as possible and at lowest cost. The three factors quality, cost and time are in tension with one another and changing one factor is likely to have an effect on the other two:

- to reduce time and maintain quality will result in increased costs;

- to reduce time and constrain costs will result in poor quality;

- to operate within reasonable costs and achieve high quality requires a significant amount of time.

The relative importance of these factors will vary from project to project.

Rapid Application Development

One approach is Rapid Application Development (RAD). There is no industry standard definition of Rapid Application Development, but it is generally taken to be the development of a 'minimum' system as quickly as possible, usually through the extensive use of prototyping.

Rapid Application Development relies on very active user participation, powerful development tools and prototyping to implement focused scopes of development as quickly as possible. Prototyping and active user participation allow the business representatives to visualise the functionality and consider the implications on the business in general. In addition, a development time constraint (Time Box) encourages the team (both users and developers) to focus on the critical and most valuable aspects of the system and avoid developing anything of little real business benefit.

The implementation of the initial project can then be followed by the development of other areas.

RAD can be typically used for projects where the system can be built within 3–6 months and advanced development tools, including prototyping tools, are available. The approach requires a small development team and users willing and able to participate in the process.

The technique of Joint Application Development (JAD) is often used in a RAD project and involves joint workshops, led by a facilitator, where IT representatives and business users jointly define the system requirements. This allows the business users to identify issues, resolve conflicts and define and prioritise requirements. For this to be successful the users must be empowered to represent their business roles thus avoiding the time-consuming process of analysts conducting a series of interviews and feedback sessions.

SSADM can be tailored to fit within a RAD environment by selecting from the techniques within the System Development Template and together with a JAD and/or timebox approach.

9.2.2 Project Start-Up and Initiation

The first step or stage of any project should be Project Start-Up and Initiation. At Project Start-Up and Initiation, the organisation and staffing of the project can be agreed and the infrastructure put in place to ensure smooth running of the project.

A typical Project Start-Up and Initiation stage will involve:

- establishing the precise scope and boundaries of the project;

- analysing risks, costs and benefits;

- determining the tasks and products required to complete the project successfully.

During this stage, an initial customisation of SSADM will be done based upon the type of project and other factors described in the section 9.4. It is strongly recommended that any customisation of SSADM is documented, describing why customisation has been considered desirable, what parameters were used to customise and any additional risks that may be incurred as a result of using the customised version.

The precise activities and products of Project Initiation will depend upon the situation. Where the terms of reference are unclear, there may be more work required than if the project has been identified as part of a strategy or programme of projects.

A typical set of activities for Project Start-Up and Initiation are:

- Project Start-Up;
    - Establish basis for project
    - Decide Project Organisation
- Project Initiation;
    - Investigate Risks, Costs and Benefits
    - Develop Project Plans.

These areas are expanded in the following sub-sections

Establish Basis for Project

Some initial analysis should be undertaken as input to detailed estimating and planning and as the basis for approval to proceed to the next stage of the project.

Some of the areas that should be established include:

- what resources are available;

- scope and boundaries – size and complexity;

- precise objectives.

Any source documents for the project should be reviewed, such as reports from strategy studies, user requirement documentation or results from previous projects. It is also important to identify any standards that will be applied to the project and assess their impact on the conduct of the project. Any errors or inconsistencies in the input documents that prevent the analysis proceeding as planned should be highlighted.

The areas for investigation should be identified and the methods of investigation established.

To gain some idea of the complexity and scope of the project, some initial analysis work may need to be undertaken. The techniques that are used will depend on the type of project. The SSADM techniques of Data Flow Modelling and Logical Data Modelling can be used to construct overview models of the area under investigation where appropriate. Business Activity Modelling should be used to understand the essential business activities of the areas that will be included in the investigation. Initial requirements should be documented in the Requirements Catalogue.

The SSADM products that will be useful at this stage include:

- Context Diagram;

- Current Physical Data Flow Diagram (Level 1);

- Overview Logical Data Structure;

- Requirements Catalogue;

- Business Activity Model.

Decide Project Organisation

In many cases, the project organisation will be standard for an organisation in terms of the roles that need to be fulfilled. However, it is worth reviewing this at the outset of a project and ensuring the project organisation is appropriate for this specific project.

Once the organisation has been decided, it is necessary to nominate individuals who will be able to take on one or more of the required roles.

Within SSADM projects, it is essential to identify the target users for the system, and establish how they are to be involved in the analysis. The user representatives should be briefed accordingly.

Investigate Risks, Costs and Benefits

All projects will be subject to technical, business and security risks that may cause delayed completion, cost overruns or poor quality deliverables. It is useful to try to identify major risks at the outset of a project so that countermeasures can be considered.

An impact assessment should be undertaken to identify the changes that may be required within the organisation as a result of the introduction of the new system in order to gain a fuller understanding of risks and costs.

A Cost/Benefit Analysis (possibly in the form of a formal Investment Appraisal) will help to decide whether it is worth proceeding with the project as it was first envisaged. At this stage, costs and benefits can only be determined approximately but establishing a good business case is an important part of managing projects.

Develop Project Plans

Once the basis of the project has been agreed, the project plan can be developed.

The project products can be identified, based on the standard set of SSADM products. The Structural Model for the project can be constructed based on the Default SSADM Structural Model.

The precise format of the project plans will depend upon local standards. Some overview guidance on project planning is given under the heading 'Planning' below.

9.2.3 Planning

A plan is a commitment to meet identified targets for products, timescales, costs, and quality. In order to define this commitment, a plan must include a range of essential information and lay down a number of essential activities.

The plans for an SSADM project should:

- define the products of each Module and of the entire project;
- chart the activities needed to produce each product;
- specify how quality will be controlled;
- define resource requirements;
- define timescales;
- display the cost profile;
- identify and allocate responsibility;
- provide a means of establishing team and individual objectives;
- facilitate control and identify control points;
- facilitate project communication.

Basis for planning

The PRINCE2 method recommends a product-based approach to planning. This means that all products of the project should be identified from the outset and plans should be constructed on the basis of the activities and resources required to complete the products. The following can be produced as an aid to this type of planning:

- **Product Breakdown Structure**. The starting point for product-based planning is a Product Breakdown Structure. The Product Breakdown Structure shows a hierarchical breakdown of all the products required by the project, both as final deliverables and as working products in the analysis, design and development process. Products are grouped according to their use: management products, quality products and specialist products. A model Product Breakdown Structure for the normal set of deliverable products required for a project using SSADM is given in Chapter 11 of this volume;

- **Product Flow Diagram**. Each product or product grouping defined on the Product Breakdown Structure can be placed in the context of other products with an indication of the dependencies between them;

- **Product Descriptions**. Each product is described by a Product Description (PD). Default Product Descriptions for the SSADM products may be found in the appropriate volume within the Business System Development series. The detail of Product Descriptions will be influenced by installation standards and procedures but may contain the following:

  - purpose;

  - composition;

  - derivation;

  - quality criteria.

- **Activity Network**. An Activity Network is created to define the actual sequence and dependencies for the technical and quality activities. Once the activities are in this logical sequence timescales can be estimated. The work can be scheduled and resources allocated. A Structural Model which covers the SSADM Modules should be used as an input to this activity. A Default Structural Model is given in Chapter 12 but this should be modified as a result of customisation of SSADM to the project. It shows how the products are derived from each other in a logical series of transformations. Each transformation acts upon one set of products to create another set.

Levels of Plan

Plans can be produced at several levels:

- the Project Plan shows the major technical activities of the whole project, and the resources required;

- the Stage Plan which covers the specific activities within a Management Stage.

The basic elements of a plan

Plans for Project and Stage will have a similar structure, at different levels of detail. Some of the standard elements of each type of plan are described below.

Plan Narrative

There should be sufficient supporting information to fully explain the plan and the narrative may contain the following:

- **Description**. This provides supporting narrative for these technical planning documents and for the other parts of the plan, details responsibilities, control tolerances and methods for monitoring and reporting performance and describes the quality control strategy.

- **Assumptions**. The management and technical assumptions which support a plan are included so that it is clearly recorded. Thus if deviations occur, the assumptions will help to ensure that the most appropriate action is taken.

- **External dependencies**. The plan shows whether the project depends on events or resources which are not within the control of the project team. For example:

  - dependencies on other projects;

  - other project(s) depending on this project;

  - a dependency on the outcome of a review (e.g., Security) encompassing several projects.

- **Prerequisites**. The successful implementation of the plan will frequently depend on certain prerequisites being met. Typically, these will be matters outside the control of the project manager or module manager, but will still need highlighting to ensure they are monitored.

- **Business risks**. There may be potential threats to the business regarding completion of the project and hence the successful implementation of the plan. These should all be identified, as far as possible.

Graphical summary

This is a graphical representation which is generally a bar or Gantt chart.

Accompanying Documents

A plan will be accompanied by appropriate supporting documents, such as a Product Breakdown Structure, Product Descriptions, Activity Network and Activity Descriptions.

9.2.4 Quality Management

In order to ensure that products are of the required quality, appropriate action must be taken at the planning stage and throughout the delivery of the project.

The project's approach to quality determines the desired quality of its products and how that quality will be achieved. During quality planning, account will be taken of the product level quality criteria, as found in the products' Product Descriptions, the general criteria deemed to apply to all, or most, products and the experience derived from previous projects.

The areas that should be covered when considering quality include:

- what standards will be applied, either external standards or standards which are internal to the organisation;

- whether standards are to be applied to the letter or whether specific deviations from standards are to be permitted;

- what types of quality reviews are to be applied to products and the procedures for review meetings and sign-off;

- what types of error correction techniques are to be applied, for example, testing, parallel running.

Quality planning results can be incorporated as elements of the plans at every level of planning as part of the plan narrative. Alternatively, some projects produce a separate Quality Plan which is less volatile in nature than the other project plans.

Each of the SSADM steps represents a transformation which takes a starting set of products, performs some tasks, and applies quality control to produce a target set of products. Quality management procedures are not part of SSADM, but each of the SSADM products that transports information between steps has quality criteria defined as part of the Product Description. These quality criteria are only those that can be applied to the individual products. Project managers should consider including an activity at the end of each stage to completely review all products that are to be delivered from that stage (excluding transient products which have been produced and superseded within the stage). This activity would be in addition to quality reviews for individual products and would aim to check that the products of the stage are complete and consistent when taken as a whole.

9.2.5 Monitoring and Control

Control must be applied to a project to make sure that the project maintains its:

- business integrity by being on schedule and within its resource and cost plans;

- technical integrity with all the products meeting their specified quality criteria as defined in their Product Descriptions.

In order to achieve control, it is necessary to monitor achievement within a project. This can be done by tracking the consumption of resource and the completion of products.

Control is exercised by comparing actual against planned achievement and then taking appropriate action. Planned achievement includes the required quality of products. The aim is to detect problems early while they can be corrected easily. Action should be taken in respect of any deviation from plan that is outside the allowed tolerance.

Control Points

Control points are necessary to ensure that, for each level of the organisation, the higher level of management can:

- monitor progress;

- compare achievement with the plan;

- detect problems;

- initiate corrective action;

- ensure that all products are produced at an adequate level of quality.

Control at different levels

The project board has responsibility for developing a system which satisfies users' requirements. This responsibility is common to all members of the project organisation. The scope and responsibility of the different levels of organisation are reflected in the different levels of plan.

Management controls are the responsibility of the project board, project manager and module manager, assisted by members of the project assurance team. Occasionally, those assisting in management control may be augmented by others with specific skills or responsibilities.

Some management controls are triggered by a particular event in the project, and some happen at fixed intervals defined in the Project Plan.

Control is normally exercised by means of formal meetings which ascertain status, analyse problems, decide on future activities and actions, and provide reports to various levels of management. The control process covers all aspects of resource usage, timescale and product quality.

9.3   The Business Case for SSADM

Organisations involved in systems development will have many objectives in common, although their priorities and measures of success may differ. The following is a list of commonly held objectives and the approach SSADM takes to enable these objectives to be achieved successfully.

Deliver the system to users on time

Timeliness depends on two things:

- good planning;
- good management and control.

SSADM has a modular structure which relates directly to project deliverables and helps in all aspects of project management. It gives a clear specification of what is to be produced and how it is to be managed and reviewed. There are well defined interfaces to management and specialist techniques.

Deliver systems that meet users' needs

By continuously involving users, by modelling business activities and work practice, by using prototyping, by making the IT professional's thinking visible through diagrammatic techniques, SSADM enhances the prospects for success on large or small projects.

Deliver systems which respond to changes in the business environment

SSADM helps in several ways here. Business Activity Modelling and Work Practice Modelling ensure that the focus of the project is on what the business requires. The system documentation produced makes visible:

- business objectives;

- practitioners' thinking and understanding of the business objectives;

- the links between the needs of the business and the system under development;

- a precise specification for the design, building, maintenance and enhancement of applications;

SSADM precisely describes what has been captured in an advanced application development environment and can be applied on projects where the target environments include 3GL, 4GL, Client/Server, distributed systems, web technology and many more.

Improve the effective and economic use of the skills available

SSADM uses the most commonly available skills in a wide market place – for example, Data Flow Modelling, Logical Data Modelling and structure diagramming. It promotes their effective use by aiding forward planning, and building up the skills base in the organisation and on particular projects. SSADM assumes the use of automated support such as CASE tools.

Improve quality by reducing error rates

Quality can be improved by detecting errors early in the life cycle, especially by involving users as well as skilled practitioners in checking for errors. Rigorous techniques promote accuracy, with extensive checks of completeness and consistency. By defining the required quality of design documents, and stating the tests for them, SSADM promotes better quality management and facilitates adoption of ISO 9001.

Improve flexibility

Every application development project is different. Project management with SSADM must cover the definition of critical success factors for the project, and be able to identify the key requirements for a successful customisation of SSADM. The ability to tailor SSADM to suit different projects is a major factor for organisations who wish to re-use their resource skills on other projects, and to be able to benefit from the many different ways in which SSADM techniques and products may be applied.

SSADM contains specific guidance on tailoring the method for particular project circumstances. SSADM defines the activities to produce standard products. With experienced technical management, the resource effort can be concentrated on producing the most critical products.

Improve productivity

Major boosts to productivity performance are achieved by:

- providing well-documented techniques which accurately specify business and system requirements. Because the method is teachable and understandable, practitioners will have a better chance of 'getting it right first time';

- defining what is needed in automated support tools – both in support for SSADM's techniques and for the generation of code in the construction of systems – software technology productivity gains can be exploited;

- using a product-oriented approach, avoiding the need to undertake unnecessary tasks, or to produce documentation at unnecessary levels of detail;

- using techniques to make thinking visible at each step;

- promoting the specification of quality criteria.

Avoid lock-in to a single source of supply

The best technical answer today may not be the best tomorrow, particularly in the field of hardware and software. The separation of logical system specification and physical design helps to establish a new layer of portability. It reduces the cost of re-implementing the system on new hardware and/or software.

SSADM services are available from a wide choice of IS service providers offering accredited training, qualified consultancy and support tools. Projects are not locked in to a single source of supply.

Avoid IT developers' bureaucracy

SSADM has been designed to provide useful tools for project managers and to transfer expertise to practitioners. Its use makes benefits, as well as costs, visible to both business and IT management and users.

9.4 Customising SSADM

SSADM is intended to be customised. SSADM defines:

- products;

- techniques;

- a Default Structural Model.

These are based on a set of underlying assumptions about project objectives, type of application and target implementation environment. SSADM will need to be customised, either because some of these assumptions do not apply or to adjust the method to the specific detail of the project.

SSADM has flexibility and an open architecture built in. However, there are characteristics which are fundamental to the method's rationale and integrity. These need to be understood if the viability of the customised method is to be maintained and conformance with SSADM principles is to be assured. No standard SSADM feature should be discarded without reason.

9.4.1 Inherent characteristics of SSADM

Although SSADM is flexible, it does have a number of characteristics that are significant to its essential consistency and integrity. Such characteristics should be retained within any customised version of SSADM in order to protect the quality of the method and hence of the project to which it is applied.

Fundamental concepts

The fundamental concepts of SSADM comprise:

- the central role of the Logical Data Model. It is essential for a project to develop a Logical Data Model as the majority of SSADM techniques are based upon this model of data. Without a Logical Data Model, SSADM cannot be used effectively;

- the event concept. Events and enquiries are the triggers to essential processes which use data from the Logical Data Model. The definition of events and enquiries should be independent of the way in which the system is packaged for presentation to users. Events and enquiries are grouped into functions which are designed to reflect the needs of the user organisation;

- the separation of the system design into Conceptual Model, External Design and Internal Design, using the Three-schema Specification Architecture. The Logical Data Model and events/enquiries are considered essential components of the Conceptual Model which reflects the underlying data and processes of the system, independent of their presentation to the user. The External Design represents the interface between the user organisation and the Conceptual Model. The Internal Design is a mapping of the Conceptual Model onto database processes.

These concepts must be preserved in any customised version of SSADM.

Essential techniques

The essential techniques within any version of SSADM, whether customised or default are:

- Logical Data Modelling;

- Entity Behaviour Modelling;

- Conceptual Process Modelling;

- Requirements Definition;

- User Interface Design.

The key products from these techniques are:

- the Logical Data Model (LDM);

- event and enquiry processing, represented by Effect Correspondence Diagrams (ECDs) and Enquiry Access Paths (EAPs);

- the Requirements Catalogue;

- User Interface Design.

9.4.2 Default project assumptions

Default SSADM has a number of stated and implicit assumptions regarding the development projects on which it is designed to be used. If any of these assumptions are invalid for a particular project then it will probably be necessary to customise SSADM for the project. Even if all these assumptions hold, there may still be reasons why customising SSADM is desirable.

Please note that these assumptions are not fundamental to SSADM – even where most of the assumptions do not apply, there is no implication that SSADM is less applicable to a project. These assumptions are used simply to highlight the possible need for modifications to be made to the Default Structural Model or to the way in which 'standard' SSADM techniques are applied in practice. This customisation is a natural part of planning any project.

The default SSADM assumptions are:

- the information to be managed by the projected system has sufficient structure to be modelled; a stable, overview Logical Data Structure can be drawn;

- the procedures to be carried out by the projected system have sufficient structure to be modelled; a high level Data Flow Diagram can be drawn for those parts of the system;

- there is a clear scope for the application; a Context Diagram can be drawn;

- there is a well-defined project initiation document;

- the project is big enough to be managed as a separate project, yet small enough to avoid partitioning into sub-projects;

- the Logical Data Model is not constrained to fit with a corporate data model, or to integrate functionally with other application systems (other than through file passing interfaces);

- substantial existing functionality is to be carried forward into the new system, with known problems to be resolved and some desired improvements of existing services;

- there is to be some new functionality;

- the projected system will maintain its own database;

- there is sufficient freedom in information systems strategy, corporate policies and organisational procedures, together with a range of non-mandatory requirements, to require a range of business options to be considered;

- there is sufficient freedom in procurement policy and technical standards to require a range of technical options to be considered;

- there are sufficient project resources, particularly in the technical areas of analysis and design, to follow the default method specification.

9.4.3 *General approach to customisation*

Generally an SSADM customisation strategy will be a component of some broader strategy which affects the way in which projects are undertaken. This chapter deals essentially with SSADM customisation but other strategic elements must be considered where this is necessary to put the SSADM matters in context. An overall flow chart of the SSADM customisation process within a project implementation strategy is shown in Figure 9-1.

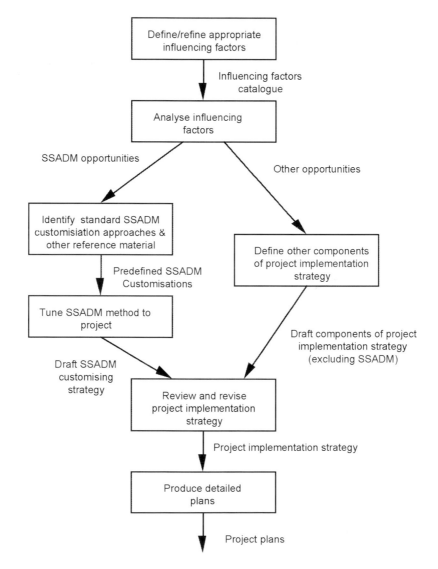

Figure 9-1 Overview of SSADM Customisation

9.4.4 Influencing factors

SSADM may be customised for the following reasons:

- to respond to specific characteristics of the application to be developed;
- to meet organisation specific constraints;
- to meet specific concerns about risk;
- to meet specific project objectives, such as, save time, reduce cost.

Some of these factors are described in the following paragraphs.

Application characteristics

The type of application being developed will be particularly significant to the SSADM customisation strategy. It has a direct impact on the scope of technical system options and the rigour (if any) which needs to be applied to particular SSADM products and techniques, such as dialogue design.

Examples of types of application system whose characteristics vary significantly from each other include:

- record keeping systems, where close synchronisation with real-world events is not critical;
- static enquiry systems, which have few update events;
- data warehouse systems where there is a large amount of data to be collected and stored and the enquiries may not be known;
- web-based development where the user interface may be the guiding factor for the system;
- decision support systems (and OLAP systems), similar to static enquiry systems, except that they have additional functionality to support a user's decision-making process;
- real-time systems, where real-world behaviour is critical;
- administrative systems, which come the closest to the default assumptions of SSADM, listed earlier.

Organisational constraints

The customisation will be influenced by constraints placed upon it by the business, particularly in the following areas:

- resources, both in quantity and quality;
- strategies, including hardware and software strategies;
- policies and legislation;

- standards.

Concerns about risk

Situational factors are used to predict risks and to determine the most appropriate project strategy for their avoidance or containment. Situational factors are the properties of the problem situation under consideration which will help in the choice of approach to be taken to the project. They are used to assess each area of the project, such as the information system or the project structure, in terms of complexity and uncertainty. From this assessment, appropriate actions to reduce risks can be taken, and these actions can be included in the tasks within the project plan.

Situational factors are many and varied. The following are examples of some factors which may be relevant to a system development project:

- information system complexity: numbers of users, diversity of users;

- information system uncertainty: users' attitudes, stability of environment;

- project task complexity: project size, migration complexity;

- project structure uncertainty: dependency on sub-contractors, dependency on other projects.

One counter measure to uncertainty and complexity is to introduce elements of modularity.

Project objectives

The project may be expected to fulfil three major objectives to varying degrees:

- quality – fitness for purpose;

- save time;

- save cost.

10   OPTIONS

This chapter covers the area within SSADM known as options. Options within SSADM consists of:

- Business System Options;

- Technical System Options.

Unlike the other techniques listed in this volume the options techniques identified within this chapter as local to SSADM as such are only defined within this volume in this series.

Options form the basis of the Decision Structure in the System Development Template. The context of Business System Options and Technical System Options in the System Development Template is represented in Figure 10-1.

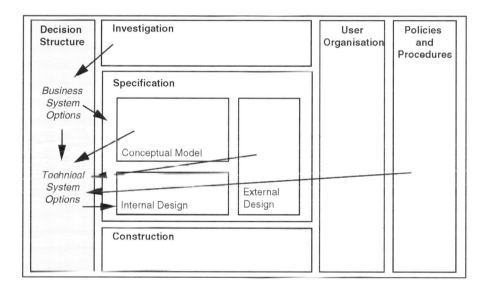

Figure 10-1 Position of Business System Options and Technical System Options in the System Development Template

Business System Options (BSOs) and Technical System Options (TSOs) are essentially points within SSADM where sufficient information has been collected about the requirements for the new system to allow the users to formally select the way forward. The type of option available to the user depends upon the amount and detail of the information available.

The 'B' and 'T' in BSO and TSO imply emphasis rather than demarcation; both have business and technical elements. As technology advances the 'T' element in BSOs is generally becoming more prominent – the way technology is used has a major impact on the business (for example, the option to allow users to take copies of data into spreadsheets to carry about on laptop computers may be balanced against the option to provide an enquiry system at the office). Some projects are primarily about exploiting technology-enabled opportunities.

'B' before 'T' reflects the priority of decision making – the major impact on the business needs to be established before dealing with the technical detail. But both sets of options are about impact on the business of the use of technology. The important issue in BSO is not to be driven by technology issues, but to describe the options from a business perspective.

10.1 Business System Options

Business System Options are the mechanism for the project team to inform the project sponsors of the alternative ways in which their system can be developed to meet their requirements and for the sponsors to make informed decisions on the way ahead. By selecting a preferred option, users take on the responsibility for ensuring that the new system will do what is required.

The formulation and selection of Business System Options is undertaken to achieve the following:

- to consolidate all of the possibilities for the overall design of the system into a manageable framework for making a choice;

- to improve the quality of the system as it is specified and designed;

- to formally agree the baseline for further development.

As indicated in Figure 10-1, Business System Options are developed with reference to the products of Investigation, principally the Requirements Catalogue. Business System Options will be greatly influenced by the Business Activity Modelling and Work Practice Modelling products. The result of the Business System Options activity is an outline of the automated part of the system that can be used to develop the products within Specification.

Development of Business System Options gives analysts and users the opportunity to explore possible changes in the system boundary.

It would not be correct to think of Business System Options as a technique that can be defined in the same way as the techniques that lie within the Investigation and Specification areas of the System Development Template. Instead, Business System Options should be viewed as an important area that needs to be covered within an SSADM project but each project must develop the approach that is most suitable for their organisation and users. This chapter describes the areas that should be covered within Business System Options, gives suggestions for products that may be developed to support the options and provides some small examples of topics that may be covered within Business System Options.

10.1.1 Business System Option Product

A Business System Option is a description of one possible solution for a proposed Information System (IS). The formulation of several Business System Options and subsequent selection of one assists the analysts and users to form a picture of the new system. Business System Options will provide the analysts with a starting point for the specification of the required system and the users with an initial overview of the system they will be receiving.

The major output of the technique will be a textual description of the selected Business System Option; this may be supported by Data Flow Diagrams (DFDs), Logical Data Structures (LDSs) and Work Practice Models. The use of these different techniques depends upon the nature and extent of the options being considered.

The textual description is an essential part of the Business System Option product; it should include references to the following:

- system boundary including a description of all the proposed functionality, cross-referenced with the Logical Data Flow Model, Business Activity Model, Requirements Catalogue and User Catalogue entries;

- levels of functionality, how well the entire application and its components are intended to function;

- Cost/Benefit Analysis;

- Impact Analysis on existing information systems, the infrastructure and the business area;

- any technical considerations that emerge as a result of Business System Option selection;

- reasons for the selection of this particular Business System Option;

- base constraints.

In addition to the textual description of the Business System Option, Data Flow Diagrams, Logical Data Structures and Work Practice Models can be used to enrich the description.

10.1.2 The Business System Option technique

There are no prescriptive guidelines for developing Business System Options. To a large extent, the approach used to formulate and present options to users will be specific to projects or organisations. Here, an approach is suggested as a basis for approaches adopted on projects. In the following paragraphs, some ideas are given on how options can be derived from the Business Activity Modelling and Work Practice Modelling products. Following that, an approach is given for formulating options, presenting them to users for selection and documenting the selected option.

Derivation from Business Activity Model and Work Practice Model

A Business Activity Model is developed as part of Investigation (scc Figure 10-1). Where a Business Activity Model exists, Business System Options should be based on the possible automation of business activities and the assignment of business activities to user roles.

Options that exist in relation to a Business Activity Model are as follows:

- automation of business activities;
- user organisations to which business activities may be assigned;
- mode of interaction between user and the automated system;
- interfaces with other automated systems/resources.

These are closely related to the mapping of business activities onto the user organisation that is done within Work Practice Modelling. They are described further in the following paragraphs.

In addition to those factors listed above, the Business Activity Model should contain a definition of scheduling constraints and business rules. The implications of these two areas will also need to be considered in the formulation of Business System Options.

Automation of business activities

In most systems there will be possibilities for automating some of the activities in the Business Activity Model. These possibilities should be considered in the formulation of options. There may be some activities that could be partially or wholly automated, depending upon the user's preference and costs. Different options should include these different possibilities to allow the user to consider what will be the best way ahead.

In the EU-Rent example, the allocation of specific cars to rental bookings can be partially automated if required by the user. For example, the rules for allocating cars to customers that might be automated include:

- allocate cars to high-tariff car groups before low-tariff car groups;
- within any car group, if there is unallocated capacity, keep 10% of the branch quota for possible walk-ins on the following day;
- compare demand for a car group at branch with available cars of that group; if there is insufficient supply, allocate spare capacity of the next higher group (i.e., providing a free 1-group upgrade), subject to retaining walk-in capacity;
- give priority for free upgrades to customers in the benefit scheme.

More complex cases could be handled by user staff.

There may be some business activities that are already automated, or partially automated, in the current system. In this case, options may need to explore the possibility of automating a larger or smaller proportion of each of the business activities under consideration.

When business activities are automated, business rules will need to be built into the automated system. Depending on the complexity of the activity, there would normally be a proportion of easily automatable rules that cover most cases. For a smaller proportion of cases, more complex rules may be required. Where this situation exists, there will be a trade-off between:

- providing automated support for business rules;
- the cost of capturing the rules and developing programs to apply them and to support their updating.

The formulation of Business System Options should acknowledge this trade-off and give the user the choice of a simple system where most rules are applied by the users and a more complex (and costly) system which applies the business rules automatically.

There are two points to note about the automation of business activities:

- many of the options for automation will have been narrowed during Requirements Definition;
- automation of activities that are currently undertaken manually implies a change in the numbers of user staff and the skills they will require.

User organisations to which business activities may be assigned

Within Business Activity Modelling it is recommended that the Business Activity Model be developed without regard to the organisation structure. This allows the Business Activity Model to be preserved through organisational changes. The Business Activity Model is mapped to a specific organisation structure in the Work Practice Model.

Restructuring at the enterprise level is outside the scope of SSADM (and is unlikely to be related to a single SSADM project). But within local areas there is usually some scope for different user roles and responsibilities.

For example, in EU-Rent:

- currently, branch counter staff take advance telephone bookings. This causes customer dissatisfaction in two ways – customers at the counter resent having their transaction interrupted while a telephone customer takes higher priority; customers who telephone get frustrated if it takes a long time for the telephone to be answered because all the counter staff are busy. One possibility is to define a separate user role for taking telephone bookings. This role could be assigned to branch counter staff, or could be assigned to a different grade of staff who would need less training than counter staff, since they would have narrower responsibilities. Such staff could be at branches or at separate locations (perhaps a national reservations office, with a freephone number, for each country in which EU-Rent operates) or both;

- currently, transfers of cars between branches are negotiated between individual branch managers. This has resulted in wasted capacity and some business lost unnecessarily – managers tend to talk to other managers with whom they have successfully co-operated in the past, and they don't have time to talk to managers of all branches within feasible transfer distance. One option for resolving this problem is to have a centralised database of all car stocks. When a branch manager requires additional cars, he/she can interrogate the automated system first to find where there may be spare capacity. This may be followed by a phone call, e-mail message or a computer-generated message to the appropriate manager to arrange the transfer. Alternatively, there could be a regional resource manager (possibly the manager of one of the larger branches). The regional manager could be responsible for all car movements between branches within his/her region and all managers may be directed to contact the regional manager to arrange car transfers on their behalf.

These examples are all about options for user roles. The automated system has to support the requirements of the user roles as defined within the organisation. However, the issue is rarely clear cut in that users and user roles can rarely be considered in isolation from the automated system being developed. The ability to define roles and their responsibilities may often be dependent upon the feasibility of providing effective support by the automated system.

Mode of interaction between user and the automated system

Information support may be provided by the automated system in one of two ways:

- in response to a user-initiated request;

- automatically, either by schedule or when specified conditions occur.

In addition to this, support may be delivered interactively or by batch reports.

The type of system which responds only to requests by users for information is likely to be very much simpler than the one which is required to respond to other types of trigger. The latter has the advantage of reducing human error but the former has the advantage of simplicity and lower cost.

The cost-benefit trade-off for these types of option may have significant effects on work practice, especially in the way user activity is scheduled.

Interfaces with other automated systems/resources

The Business Activity Model includes an analysis of information which is provided from and to the wider system. Where the information flowing across the boundary is used or generated by a business activity which is to be automated, there may be a need to consider whether an automated interface is required and if so, what form it should take.

The automated systems/resources which may require interfaces include:

- other computer systems in the organisation or other applications running on the same computer system. Options here should consider whether direct interfaces are required or whether transfer of data should be via some form of magnetic media such as disk or tape. Direct interfaces have the advantage of reducing the need for user interaction but require more sophisticated validation routines and data transfer programs. Interfaces via magnetic media are more easy to control and are usually cheaper to implement;

- IT-based services available to the users, but not designed with SSADM. For example:

  - workstation-based tools such as PC databases and spreadsheets: some of the reports produced by the SSADM-developed system will be required in electronic form for loading into such tools;

  - office products, such as e-Mail, group diaries, employee time recording systems. Are interfaces required between them and the SSADM-developed system?

  - external information services, such as credit card validation, weather and road condition reports. In the EU-Rent system, counter staff may phone the credit card companies to check credit ratings or use an automatic link to a centralised credit computer from the SSADM-developed system.

- external IT systems, such as credit card debiting. Within EU-Rent, options would be to send paper vouchers to credit card companies or have a counter terminal through which the credit card is 'swiped' for direct input through to an automated system. The choice then is whether to produce a magnetic file, or send direct transactions from within SSADM-developed dialogues.

Development of each Business System Option

Coverage of options

A spectrum of options should be developed, each of which satisfies all the mandatory requirements listed in the Requirements Catalogue. In general, three options are usually adequate to present the different alternatives open for selection by the user. It is useful to develop a 'minimum' and 'maximum' option and one in between:

- the 'minimum' option meets all of the mandatory requirements, and a minimal number of important requirements. The facilities offered in this option should be unsophisticated and low-cost, for example, the option for information support might consist of user-initiated reports rather than more sophisticated information support triggered by schedules or combinations of circumstances. This option should not go to the extreme of proposing a solution which will obviously not gain user acceptance;

- the 'maximum' option meets the important and nice-to-have requirements as well as the mandatory requirements. This option should generally not exceed the upper limits on cost and timescale for the project but should attempt to present to the user the most sophisticated option that might be considered practical;

- the 'in-between' option represents a balanced view offering a solution somewhere between the 'maximum' and 'minimum' options, possibly offering features not covered by the other two options. This option should attempt to demonstrate some of the trade-offs between the low-cost of the 'minimum' option and the sophistication of the 'maximum' option, aiming to demonstrate the value of various features when compared to their cost.

In formulating the options, it is useful to consider to what degree the new system will match the business activities within the organisation. For example, will all the business events of the Business Activity Model be recognised as individual events? Is all the data required by each business activity stored and retrieved from the automated system or is it only a sub-set? For example, in EU-Rent there are several business events which cause a customer to be denoted as 'dead' (customer death, customer bankruptcy, management decision to cease business relationship with customer) whereas the automated system may simply need to know about 'customer removal', possibly accompanied by a reason. Also, it is worth considering how up-to-date the data will be in the automated system compared with the real-world data it represents. Sometimes, it is necessary for the automated system to be completely up-to-date as in an airline booking system. In other situations, it is adequate for data to be a day or even a week out of date as it is only interrogated on a period-by-period basis.

It is unlikely that there will be a number of clear cut options completely different from one another. Instead, the variations are more likely to be in small system areas, general facilities or levels of what is available. The sort of problem capable of being explored while developing a Business System Option is that of conflicting priorities and objectives. An example of this dilemma is whether a system offers ease of use and access in the knowledge that this must involve sacrifice of security. Accordingly, it is not possible to be prescriptive about the form of the options. They must be expressed in text, but can use Data Flow Diagrams, Logical Data Structure or Work Practice Model to expand the description. It is important that the Business System Options can be understood by their target audience. The level of description must be such that users can readily understand it.

Common features of options

There are features that will be common to each Business System Option:

- the establishment of a list of minimum requirements to which all Business System Options must conform;

- the identification of the boundary and scope of each Business System Option;

- the identification of users and their tasks.

Interfaces to other systems

Interfaces to other Information Systems – either internal or external – should be considered. These interfaces will be identified either from the Business Activity Model or from the Logical Data Flow Model. How interfaces to other organisations and systems will be managed should be explored as discussed above.

Cost/Benefit Analysis

A Cost/Benefit Analysis should accompany each option. It will not be possible to calculate precise costs for each option; however, it should be possible to use rough estimates for comparison purposes. In considering the costs and benefits of each option it should be noted that there is often a trade-off between sophistication and usability. The more sophistication, the greater the impact but the potential benefits are likely to be greater.

Description of organisation and user roles

A description of the new system organisation can be included as part of the Business System Option. This will document the distribution of responsibilities amongst different user roles.

Technical/Technology considerations

Technical considerations should be included in a Business System Option if they have impact on the business or on system functionality.

Some of the possibilities for the implementation of the required support are likely to be a mix of:

- designed system, possibly developed as a mixture of package and bespoke software;

- bought-in technology such as e-mail, query processors, word processors and spreadsheets;

- bought-in data or services such as a gazetteer provided by the Post Office detailing all streets and postcodes in the UK or map and routing packages.

The right mix of technologies and development approaches need to be determined during Business System Options. These issues are legitimate for presentation and selection at this early stage as they will affect the way in which the system is specified and integrated into the business. The precise technical details can be dealt with during Technical System Options.

Scheduling of Delivery

Business System Options may address the way in which a system is to be delivered as well as the basic facilities to be provided. There may be a subset of requirements satisfied by the first delivery of the system with further requirements being satisfied by later deliveries. At this point, it may not be possible to be precise about the exact content of particular phases, but the presentation of options in this area should help the users to decide their overall requirements regarding the delivery of the system.

In the EU-Rent system, one option may be to provide basic information support in the first phase of delivery with later phases automating business rules. Another option could be to deliver support for a limited range of business activities in the first phase with subsequent phases providing support for other business activities.

Selection of Business System Option

For larger systems with a wide variety of user types, selection may take some time and require a significant amount of work.

Although it is called 'selection', in reality it is often creation of the requirements baseline. The options presented define the scope of negotiation, not 'take it or leave it' choices. What is actually selected should be within the defined spectrum, but may not match any of the options presented very closely.

What is presented is not the whole story. It should be backed up by knowledge, gathered in Requirements Definition and Business Activity Modelling, about different possibilities for meeting requirements. This should be introduced into the debate on the option to be selected.

The selection of options is carried out by the users, either the project board itself or a review body with powers delegated to it by the project board. The Business System Options will be presented to the review body by the systems analysts. The reviewers must be given enough information to convey meaning, but not so much that they are swamped in details.

It is at this point that the users can decide that the project will be unable to deliver the anticipated benefits within the estimated costs. The extreme resolution of this situation will be to abandon further work on the project.

Steps in selection

There are four steps in the selection process:

- prepare presentations;
- make presentations;
- provide amplification and answer queries;
- record selection decisions.

A wide range of skills, not especially associated with SSADM, but which result from systems analysis experience and training, will be required here. The systems analyst will use these to plan, prepare and execute the presentation and decision-making process. The Business System Options will be presented by the analyst who will explain their strengths and weaknesses, coordinate the decisions and obtain agreement.

In some situations, it may be considered useful to develop prototypes of some areas of the system to demonstrate what is being proposed.

Making the selection

The users need to be presented with options so that they can decide upon their priorities and needs.

The users are the people who will be affected by or benefit from the new system, some of whom will have responsibilities for the business area to which the new system is intended to add value. Business System Option selection will give them opportunities to learn what an automated system can do for them. It should also enable them to have a greater degree of insight into their own requirements. Developing and selecting Business System Options should show users what is possible but not restrict them to pre-determined ideas. Because there will be a range of users from decision makers and 'purse holders' to end-user operators, each with different responsibilities, the analyst will need to exercise judgement in order to decide which particular users will be able to provide the specific information required.

The impacts on the organisation need to be explained carefully for each option to help in the decision-making process. The presentation of Business System Options should be relatively easily understood by the users as the Business System Options are set at the level of how things will need to be organised. When the options are discussed with the users, they may wish to add suggestions of their own or ask for more options to be produced. Finally, the agreed way forward may incorporate features from a number of the options as well as new ideas generated during discussions.

Documenting the selection

The selection should be agreed and then documented. The selected option will almost inevitably be an amalgam of several of the options put to the project board. The reasons for its selection and any significant reasons for not selecting any of the other options must be recorded together with the description of the chosen option. This description must incorporate any changes to it or the supporting documentation resulting from Business System Option selection.

10.1.3 Relationship with other analysis and design techniques

Requirements Definition

The requirements of the new system recorded in the Requirements Catalogue provide the basis for the creation of Business System Options. The selected Business System Option, in turn, is likely to highlight changes required to entries in the Requirements Catalogue. These changes will take the form of adding new requirements identified during Business System Option development and annotating requirements not included in the selected Business System Option with reasons for their non-selection.

Data Flow Modelling

The Logical Data Flow Model can be used as a source for Business System Option creation and the Required System Data Flow Model is created in the context of the selected Business System Option. Outline Data Flow Diagrams may be created to assist in the development and presentation of the Business System Options.

Logical Data Modelling

The Current Environment Logical Data Model can be used as a source for Business System Option creation. The Required System Logical Data Model will be developed in the context of the selected Business System Option.

Work Practice Modelling

Part of Work Practice Modelling involves the creation of the User Catalogue which describes the target users and the tasks that they undertake. This information provides a context in which Business System Option creation can take place. User roles may be identified during Business System Options as the mapping of business activities onto the organisation structure is considered.

Business Activity Modelling

Business activities, business events and interfaces between the business activities and the wider system are all used in the formulation and evaluation of Business System Options.

Prototyping

Prototypes of areas of the system can be developed and demonstrated as part of the formulation and presentation of Business System Options where required.

10.2   Technical System Options

Technical System Options (TSOs) will provide the outline plan for the development of the selected Business System Option (BSO).

As indicated in Figure 10-1, Technical System Options are developed as an elaboration of the selected Business System Option. One of the major inputs to the formulation of Technical System Options will be from the Policies and Procedures of the organisation and will generally cover:

- technical architecture including hardware, system software and communications configurations where these items have been determined at a strategic level;

- application architecture including size, structuring principles, interaction between applications, use of shared data and user interfaces;

- procurement including preferred hardware/software suppliers, compatibility with existing IT assets and the procedure for procurement;

- organisational standards constraining any of the above.

Technical System Options need to combine the information from the selected Business System Option and Policies and Procedures with information taken from products within the Conceptual Model and External Design to provide viable alternatives for the way ahead.

Technical System Options will address such areas as:

- a specification of the technical environment, e.g., provision and distribution of hardware devices; software environment; operating regime;

- confirmation of the functions to be done, and the manner in which they are to be carried out;

- impact of changes to the organisation and methods of working;

- impact on the development organisation and infrastructure for the remainder of the project.

Technical System Options is the mechanism by which the project manager provides the user management with specific technical information on the way forward, its costs, implications and timescales. User management will then make an informed decision, selecting the most appropriate way ahead related to their organisation and the project's objectives.

The selected Technical System Option will provide the Technical System Architecture (TSA) which is the specification for the physical environment for input to Physical Design (including Internal Design).

10.2.1 Skills required for Technical System Options

The skills required for the development of Technical System Options are far beyond the skills required for analysis and design. In order to develop feasible options, it is necessary for the team to have an understanding of a wide range of technical issues.

Important non-SSADM skills include:

- knowledge of capabilities of technology, what is available in the market (and what else is coming soon), what is realistic;

- knowledge of how technologies fit together – DBMS, TP software, communications, user interface managers, 'bought-in' technology such as e-mail and personal computer packages (word processing, spreadsheets, etc.);

- IT systems sizing and capacity planning;

- hardware and software procurement ;

- cost-benefit analysis.

Ideally, these skills should be found in members of the development team. If not, the team will need to bring in expertise or be given access to specialists.

One source of details for skills requirements is SFIA which is the white paper on Skills Framework for the Information Age. This is recommended for use by all government departments has been built to describe IT/IS job roles by the IT National Training Organisation (ITNTO).

10.2.2 Products of Technical System Options

The SSADM products of Technical System Options before selection will be:

- several Technical System Options, each comprising:
    - Cost/Benefit Analysis;
    - Impact Analysis;
    - Outline Development Plan;
    - Technical System Architecture (in outline only);
    - System Description.

After selection:

- selected Technical System Option:
    - Outline Development Plan;
    - selection reasoning;
- Technical System Architecture;
    - Impact Analysis;
    - System Description;
- Application Style Guide.

The Technical System Option carries all the argument for a particular option, but once the selection has been made then the Technical System Architecture (enhanced from an outline for that option) will carry the decisions forward to Physical Design.

Each Technical System Option must be sufficiently detailed to enable:

- informed decisions to be made;

- the systems analyst to assist in the evaluation of the options.

The options will contain the elements described in the following paragraphs.

Technical System Architecture (TSA)

Note that before selection, the Technical System Architecture exists only in outline for each option. Only after selection of the Technical System Option does the Technical System Architecture become more detailed, and thence a distinct product.

The outline Technical System Architecture's objective is to provide sufficient information for the user to understand how the system will work, for significant design factors to be explained, and for detailed cost estimates to be made. It should cover the following areas:

- hardware;

- software;

- system sizing;

- additional items.

Before selection, the level of detail in these areas will be decided on a project-by-project basis. After selection, the Technical System Architecture is enhanced. It will contain all the elements previously included plus some parts of the selected Technical System Option:

- System Description;

- Impact Analysis.

All the elements of the Technical System Architecture are described in the following paragraphs.

Hardware

A description supported by a layout diagram, expanded with specific details such as types, numbers and locations of devices. Examples that may be covered are:

- standards;

- communications/networking;

- environment;

- installation;

- operations;

- upgrade arrangements;

- reliability;

- serviceability;

- availability;
- maintainability.

Software

A description carrying specific information about the actual system facilities required, the method of provision, and the quantity of application software. Typical aspects addressed could include:

- type of Database Management System (DBMS);
- development environment;
- communications software;
- system utilities required, e.g., back-up and recovery facilities;
- operating system capabilities;
- application packages;
- method of constructing applications programs, e.g., 3GL and/or 4GL;
- number of application programs.

System sizing

In order to specify both hardware and software environments it will be necessary to first carry out a system sizing exercise. This is best achieved by the use of Capacity Planning techniques . Where Capacity Planning expertise is not available, a rough estimate of system size can be calculated by the following:

- data – can be represented as a percentage of the total figure based on knowledge of the particular target hardware/software environment. This is derived by:
  - modifying the Required System Logical Data Model to support each option;
  - annotating the resulting Logical Data Model with volumes;
  - estimating data size for each entity;
  - calculating a total estimate for logical data;
  - adding in estimates for overheads (e.g., overflow, expansion, pointers, indexes).
- processing – this is more difficult to calculate. An approach could be:
  - select the Function Definitions, Effect Correspondence Diagrams, Enquiry Access Paths and I/O Structures for the option;
  - ensure that volumes and frequencies have been documented;
  - estimate average processing time for an entity update. Include time elements for overheads such as I/O, application program, TP monitor, etc.;

- ■ calculate the processing time for each function;

- ■ calculate the estimated processing load for each processing cycle by applying the volume and frequency data to the calculated event processing time;

- ■ from Function Definitions add in an estimate for processing not related to update events in each cycle (e.g., Enquiries, transaction file update, etc.);

- ■ use the Function Definitions to estimate the overheads represented by the system interfaces.

- • First-cut Physical Design – in some cases it may be necessary to produce an overview physical design. This would apply, for example, where a comparison of the physical implementation effects is required because the options are very different, or where options differ in data organisation and/or handling strategy. The requirement is to obtain enough to size the system for a Technical System Option and therefore this will not extend to the full rigour of Physical Design, but be restricted to a high level pass.

When estimating throughput, it is important to take account of waiting times for shared resources (such as disks and communications lines) as well as resource time. It is especially important to know the critical levels of load beyond which waiting times increase rapidly, and ensure that there is sufficient capacity that traffic stays below these levels for most of the time. For example, with random demand, increase of capacity from 50% to 60% typically increases average waiting time by about 50%, increase in load from 50% to 70% increases average waiting time by about 130%. Simple queuing models can be created on spreadsheets to estimate waiting times; the relevant formulae are readily available in textbooks or may be provided as standard functions within spreadsheet packages.

Additional items

To complete the Technical System Architecture, include mention of any other points which may be of significance and need to be taken into account in the selection of the option, for example:

- • fallback and recovery arrangements;

- • access rights;

- • access and security methods;

- • hardware/software maintenance.

System Description

This emphasises the changes in the functionality which had been described in the Requirements Specification. On the whole the changes will be documented in text with reference to the particular part of the Requirements Specification affected.

Impact Analysis

This is based on the Technical System Option Impact Analysis and will contain information about the decisions which directly affect the system implementation:

- user organisation and staffing for the new system, which may include the IS providers;

- outline specification of user interface procedures, and interface procedures to other systems if relevant;

- specification of the project objectives to be achieved. They are derived largely from the statements of advantages in the option specification, as quantified for the Cost/Benefit Analysis. They are required for future reference to:

  - check that the system actually achieves its expected benefits;

  - act as a check on the relevance and importance of proposed amendments.

System Description

This is included in the alternative Technical System Options and is subsumed into the Technical System Architecture for the selected Technical System Option. The System Description shows how the Requirements Specification is met by the option being specified. In many cases the major decisions in this area will have already been taken in choosing a Business System Option. In some cases, however, it may be appropriate to propose options which meet the required system to different levels, for example, trading off facilities against costs and development time.

The degree to which the system requirement is met will be shown in this description. To minimise effort in producing the description maximum use should be made of the SSADM products available, modified to reflect the option. Products that would normally be included are:

- Required System Logical Data Model;

- Function Definitions;

- Requirements Catalogue (with solutions reflecting the option).

An option's significance can be emphasised by including a list of functions/facilities not being provided to support the products mentioned above.

Impact Analysis

This explains the effects of the option on the user environment. The impact analysis is an opportune mechanism to raise particular issues which, although not directly SSADM issues, will affect the quality of the final Information System implemented. The project management will then have both the issues raised and some initial information about them. The issues are documented in the following products:

- Training Requirements Description;

- User Manual Requirements Description;

- Testing Outline;
- Take-on Requirements Description.

The remaining points to be covered may include:

- organisation and staffing;
- significant changes in user operating procedures;
- implementation considerations (e.g., conversion, the effects of staff learning curves on service levels);
- savings, in terms of replaced equipment, maintenance, etc.;
- advantages and disadvantages in comparison with the other Technical System Options.

  Advantages might include:

  - improved turnover/work rates
  - business objectives achieved
  - ease and speed of implementation
  - lower development costs
  - reliability
  - projected cost containment
  - staff savings
  - better performance and service.

  Disadvantages might be:

  - limitations on improvements
  - business objectives not achieved
  - difficulties in implementation and/or increased timescale
  - higher implementation costs
  - reduced performance.

Note that if the Technical System Architecture, as described for this option, has an impact upon the Requirements Specification then this must be highlighted. Management can then ensure that, if necessary, these implications can be passed through the Requirements Specification Module to assess the full extent of the implications.

Outline Development Plan

This outline plan provides input to the development strategy for the remainder of the project for the specific option, so that provisional timescales and resource requirements, and therefore development costs, can be estimated. From this users and project management will budget resources, and coordinate their activities. Only the next Module can be planned in detail, the plans post Physical Design will be more vague and subject to amendment.

The plan may contain the following:

- system design;
- program design and programming;
- procurement (if relevant);
- system testing;
- implementation including a plan for roll-out of the implemented system.

10.2.3 Constraints on the formulation of Technical System Options

Before starting to consider the individual options, it is advisable to be clear on the constraints which are involved in restricting the potential options open to the systems analyst.

There are two types of constraint to be considered:

- 'External' – these are imposed from outside the project
- 'Internal' – within the scope of the project, constraints in terms of the objectives and the service level requirements which have been identified and documented.

Taken together these will provide the framework within which the systems analyst can develop the options for presentation to, and selection by, user management.

External constraints

The overriding constraints should have been considered in Business System Options. The analyst should revisit the documentation defining the project's environment to establish whether any of these parameters have changed since Business System Option selection.

External constraints will apply to all options, and will therefore define the overall Technical System Option scope and framework. These constraints should already be documented/identified by the systems analyst from investigations and discussions with the relevant user(s) and management. Examples of 'external' constraints are:

- time – 'The new system must be operational by ...';
- cost – 'Total development cost of the project must not exceed £x';
- business performance versus project value – 'Must achieve an annual saving over current costs of £x within n years';
- hardware/software – 'The new system must be implemented on existing equipment and use the currently implemented DBMS';

- policies – technical architecture, application architecture and procurement policies may be constraints on the options.

It is good practice to informally review the external constraints with users to determine the degree to which any of these constraints are fixed.

Internal constraints

Internal constraints will have been documented as requirements in the Requirements Catalogue. Some areas which will constrain the Technical System Options are:

- mandatory facilities – for example, on-line access, word processing;
- minimum global service levels:
    - mean time between failures;
    - maximum time to restore system;
    - performance level of back-up system;
    - availability;
    - reliability;
    - contingency;
    - useability.
- data storage criteria derived from the Required System Logical Data Model (LDM), in terms of:
    - maximum file sizes;
    - backing storage utilisation.
- critical timing criteria from the Function Definitions, such as:
    - highest interactive peaks;
    - most critical on-line response;
    - largest transaction volumes.
- other objectives not covered above. Possibilities are:
    - operating environment conditions;
    - security requirements;
    - interfacing to other Information Systems.

10.2.4 Technical System Option development

As part of developing Technical System Options, some external investigation may be required. This will often mean collecting technical data (usually from the suppliers themselves) such as: costs, facilities, performance. This is not a question of selecting a supplier, but rather one of obtaining sufficient information to identify whether particular configurations will meet the requirements and constraints. External investigation is necessary unless the choice is constrained by policies within the organisation. This type of investigation may be undertaken by a specialist group with knowledge and experience of the types of technology that may be appropriate. Some of the parameters for the technical environment will have been set as part of Business System Options.

The number of options considered will vary from project to project. Although three is a reasonable guide, it may be found that more will need to be considered.

Developing Technical System Options

Technical System Options should aim to explore the possible implementation mechanisms for the different elements of the Three-schema Specification Architecture (the three components of the Specification area of the System Development Template).

Taking into account the constraints of technical architecture, application architecture and procurement policies, the formulation of options should explore:

- candidate technologies for the External Design, for example what style of Graphical User Interface will be used or (e.g., 'Windows' or 'Browser'). If these broad decisions have been made at an earlier stage in the project, Technical System Options should identify specific tools and equipment that will be used to develop the user interface;

- candidate technologies for Conceptual Model processes. A decision will need to made as to whether Conceptual Model processes will be tightly coupled with the Internal or External Design;

- candidate data storage and retrieval technologies;

- candidate technologies for communication between Conceptual Model, External Design and Internal Design.

For each option developed, it is necessary to ensure that:

- the combinations can work together;

- that interfaces to bought-in technologies are feasible;

- interfaces to other IT systems are feasible.

For each option developed, a Cost/Benefit Analysis should be undertaken. At the stage of Technical System Options, specific technical solutions should be proposed which can be costed more readily than the broad solutions proposed as part of Business System Options. In addition, an analysis of the impact of each solution should be considered and documented.

Selecting an option

For larger systems with a wide variety of user types, selection may take some time and require a significant amount of work. Reference may need to be made to decisions taken during Business System Options.

Although it is called 'selection', in reality it is often creation of the design baseline. The options presented define the scope of negotiation, not 'take it or leave it' choices. What is actually selected should be within the defined spectrum, but may not match any of the options presented very closely.

The selection of options is carried out by the users, either the project board itself or a review body with powers delegated to it by the project board. The Technical System Options will be presented to the review body by the systems analysts. The reviewers must be given enough information to convey meaning, but not so much that they are swamped in detail.

There are four steps in the selection process:

- prepare presentations;
- make presentations;
- provide amplification and answer queries;
- record selection decisions.

A wide range of skills, not especially associated with SSADM, but which result from systems analysis experience and training, will be required here. The systems analyst will use these to plan, prepare and execute the presentation and decision-making process. The analyst will be part of the team, lead by the project/module manager, presenting the Technical System Options, explaining their strength and weaknesses, coordinating and recording the decisions and obtaining agreement.

In some situations, it may be considered useful to develop prototypes of some areas of the system to demonstrate what is being proposed.

The users need to be presented with options so that they can decide upon their priorities and needs. As the options are very technical in nature, it would be usual for users to appoint advisers with substantial technical knowledge and expertise to assist in the evaluation and selection of options.

The impacts on the organisation need to be explained carefully for each option to help in the decision-making process. The presentation of Technical System Options should attempt to describe each option in plain terms, concentrating on the impacts, costs and benefits. The agreed way forward may incorporate features from a number of the options as well as new ideas generated during discussions.

Once the decision has been made it will be necessary to update the selected Technical System Option and its Technical System Architecture.

The selected option will be reviewed once again from the capacity planning viewpoint to ensure the service level requirements are met. If not, there will be three options:

- propose a different architecture with more capacity;
- reduce the service level requirement targets;

- propose changes to the Requirements Specification.

Whichever of these recommendations is proposed, it will have to be considered by the decision makers in order to ascertain whether an exception condition has been encountered and some rework is necessary.

10.2.5 Relationship with other techniques

Business System Options

The decisions made in Business System Options form the basis for the possibilities explored in Technical System Options. Often, an outline technical approach has been decided in Business System Options. This needs to be elaborated during Technical System Options. Where any assumptions made in Business System Options are found to be invalid during Technical System options, these should be highlighted.

Requirements Definition

The requirements from the Requirements Catalogue will form a major input into Technical System Options, in particular all non-functional requirements. Non-functional requirements will be a vital input into capacity planning and system sizing.

Physical Design

When deriving the options, thought must be given to the probable size (in data and processes) of the final system. Where rough sizing methods do not produce satisfactory estimates, then a first-cut physical design may be necessary.

The Technical System Architecture will be a major input to Physical Design.

11   PRODUCT BREAKDOWN STRUCTURE

This chapter provides a model of how products being produced within a project combine to provide full documentation of the process of analysing and designing computer applications using SSADM.

The Product Breakdown Structure (PBS) presented in this chapter is intended to provide an initial 'standard model'. It is expected that individual projects will use this model as a basis for tailoring, adding and removing products as necessary.

Within the overall Product Breakdown Structure for a project Application Products are those products which are normally associated with the development of a computer system. These products include:

- the project documentation of the analysis and design activities, in this case SSADM products;

- the working, physical system with its associated documentation.

Figure 11-1 shows the Application products for a complete development, indicating those which are considered to be within SSADM (these are broken down further in diagrams below).

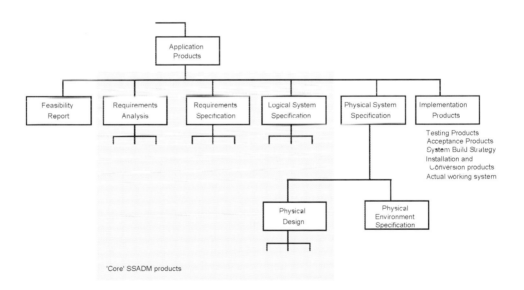

Figure 11-1 Application Products Product Breakdown Structure

Only those boxes in the shaded area are covered in more detail in this chapter. These are defined as follows:

- **Requirements Analysis** – covers the products developed as a result of the examination of any existing system, the analysis of the requirements for the new system and the setting of the boundary for the new system (Business System Options). These products correspond with those developed in Stages 1 and 2 of the SSADM Default Structural Model (see Chapter 12);

- **Requirements Specification** – covers the products developed to specify the data to be stored, the processing of the data and the user interface design for the new system. These products correspond with those developed in Stage 3 of the SSADM Default Structural Model. It is expected that the bulk of the products produced by a project using SSADM will fall into this area as this where the detailed specification of the new system is documented;

- **Logical System Specification** – covers the products developed to show the detailed design of the processing for the new system. In addition the Technical System Option products are included. These products correspond with those developed in Stages 4 and 5 of the SSADM Default Structural Model;

- **Physical Design** – covers the products developed for Database Design and Physical Process Specification. These products correspond with those developed in Stage 6 of the SSADM Default Structural Model.

The other products are described briefly as follows:

- **Feasibility Report**. This product records whether or not the users' needs can indeed be reasonably met by the proposed system;

- **Physical System Specification**. The Physical System Specification comprises the Physical Design which is merged with the detail of technical environment on which the application is to be implemented;

- **Implementation Products. Implementation** Products provide the detail necessary to set up the final working system, so that it adheres to the users' requirements. Much of the detail here will be augmented by the Operations Products, User Products and Handover Products all identified in the Product Breakdown Structure as Technical Products on the same level as Application Products.

11.1 Requirements Analysis

The Product Breakdown Structure for the Requirements Analysis is shown in Figure 11-2.

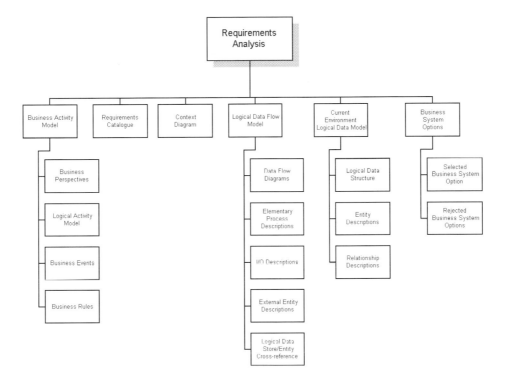

Figure 11-2 Product Breakdown Structure for Requirements Analysis

The products shown above fall into three categories as follows:

- **Products from the investigation of any current system**. These include the Business Activity Model, the Logical Data Flow Model and the Current Environment Logical Data Model;

- **Products defining the requirements for the new system**. This covers the Requirements Catalogue;

- **Products defining the scope to be covered by the new system**. This covers the Business System Options products.

It should be noted that the Current Physical Data Flow Model is not included in this set as it is regarded as an intermediate product used to develop the Logical Data Flow Model.

11.2 Requirements Specification

The Product Breakdown Structure for the Requirements Specification is shown in Figure 11-3.

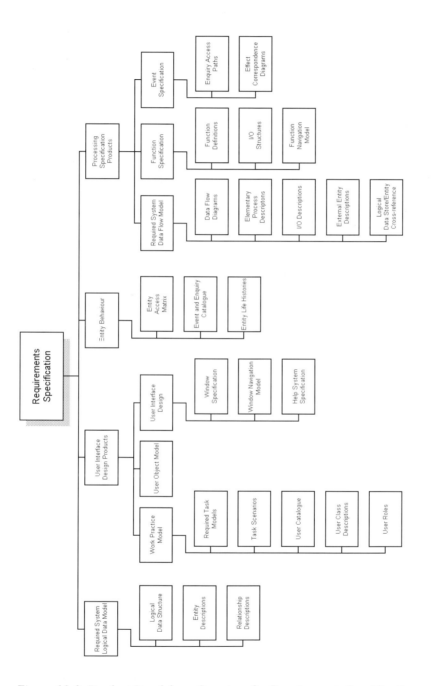

Figure 11-3 Product Breakdown Structure for Requirements Specification

The products shown above fall into four categories as follows:

- **Products used to specify the data to be held for the new system**. This covers the Required Logical Data Model products;

- **Products used to design the user interface for the new system**. These include the Work Practice Model products, the User Object Model and the User Interface Design products;

- **Products that specify how the data is changed over time**. This includes the Entity Life Histories, Entity Access Matrix and the Event and Enquiry Catalogue;

- **Products that specify what processing is required for the new system**. These include the Required System Data Flow Model products, the Function Specification products and the Event Specification products.

It should be noted that the Relational Data Analysis products do not appear in this Product Breakdown Structure as they are regarded as intermediate products used to validate the Required System Logical Data Model. Likewise the products of Prototyping and Evaluation are also regarded as being intermediate products with the results being absorbed into the other Requirements Specification products.

11.3 Logical System Specification

The Product Breakdown Structure for the Logical System Specification is shown in Figure 11-4.

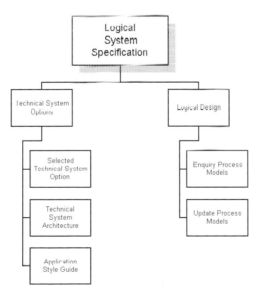

Figure 11-4 Product Breakdown Structure for Logical System Specification

The products shown above fall into two categories as follows:

- **Products used to document the chosen technical environment**. This covers the Technical System Options products;

- **Products used to specify in detail the Enquiry and Update processing**. These include the Enquiry Process Models and the Update Process Models. These products should be considered highly optional and only produced on projects that would benefit from specifications being defined in a structured manner.

11.4 Physical Design

This product is, along with the Application Development Standards, the final SSADM deliverable (from the Physical Design Module) before implementation activities commence. It includes the detailed specification of the data and processing to be implemented. The Product Breakdown Structure for the Physical Design is shown in Figure 11-5.

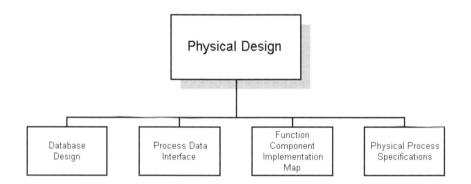

Figure 11-5 Product Breakdown Structure for Physical Design

Although the four products shown above are shown as a flat structure they can be devided into three categories as follows:

- **Products that define the physical organisation of the data**. This covers the Database Design;

- **Products that define the physical process specifications**. This covers the Physical Process Specifications and the Function Component Implementation Map;

- **Products that show the link between the data and the processing.** this covers the Process Data Interface.

12   DEFAULT STRUCTURAL MODEL

A Structural Model is a definition of the Stages and Steps that need to be undertaken on a project. SSADM is designed to be customised which means that different projects will use different versions of the Structural Model. The Structural Model described in this chapter should be used as the default for a project which is then modified to fit the particular circumstances encountered by the project.

Overview of the Structural Model

The SSADM Default Structural model is based on a series of Modules.

The modular structure is described in detail below. Figure 12-1 shows the Modules of SSADM, their constituent Stages and their products.

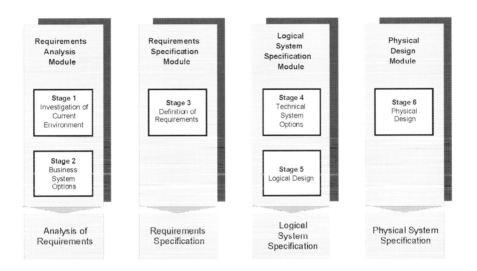

Figure 12-1 The Modules of SSADM

The products shown in Figure 12-1 are the group products which form the basis for the SSADM Product Breakdown Structure (see Chapter 11). The Structural Model defines Steps within each of the Stages.

Thus the Structural Model consists of:

- diagrams showing the structure of Steps within Stages, their interdependencies and major inputs and outputs;

- descriptions of each Step within each Stage;

- descriptions of each Stage.

12.1   Stage 1: Investigation of Current Environment

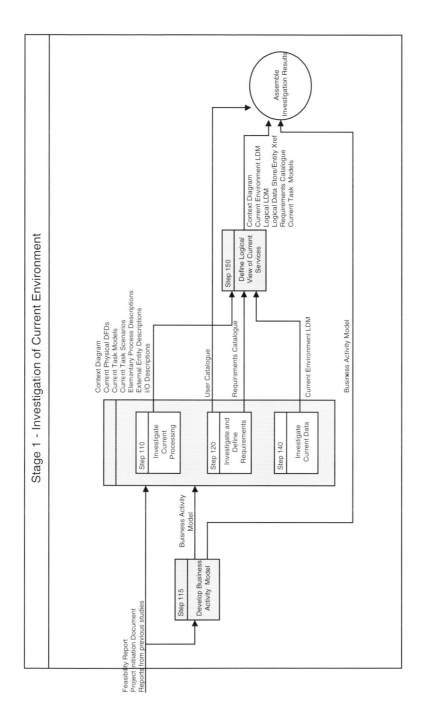

This Stage has the special characteristic of a planning step which either initiates the project, or on inspection of source documents, such as the Feasibility Report, may recommend that management reconsider the objectives in the Project Initiation Document. It is an activity of getting to know the business area and, importantly, all those who have a stake in it and their objectives. This involves the conventional analysis skills of information gathering.

From this overview, detailed requirements are collected, and models of the business are built. These models will include both existing clerical and IT systems, as well as planned business procedures and information needs.

These physical views of information and procedure are then converted to a logicalised view to produce the comprehensive survey results. These are expressed without reference to current physical constraints. All these constraints and problems are recorded, alongside other system objectives in the Requirements Catalogue.

Step 110: Investigate Current Processing

This Step investigates the information flow associated with the services currently provided, and describes them in the form of a Data Flow Model. The development of the Current Physical Data Flow Model uses information gathered for Step 120 (Investigate and Define Requirements) and proceeds in parallel with Step 140 (Investigate Current Data).

Document Flow Diagrams, Resource Flow Diagrams and a Context Diagram can be developed as an input to the development of the Current Physical Data Flow Model.

At this point the Data Flow Model represents the current services with all their deficiencies. No attempt is made to incorporate required improvements, or new facilities.

Task Models and Task Scenarios can also be developed to show the way the users interrelate with any current system.

Step 115: Develop Business Activity Model

As a precursor to a detailed investigation of the requirements for a new automated system, a model of business activities is built. Techniques for Business Activity Modelling should be drawn from well-established methods for Business Activity Modelling such as the Soft Systems Methodology. Business events and business rules should also be investigated as an input to the specification of the automated system.

Step 120: Investigate and Define Requirements

The Requirements Catalogue is developed in this step. Requirements may also be identified during the parallel development of the Current Physical Data Flow Diagrams and the Current Environment Logical Data Model in Step 130 (Investigate Current Processing) and Step 140 (Investigate Current Data) respectively.

Requirements are generally of two types: functional and non-functional. While requirements may only be described in broad terms initially, efforts should be made to ensure that, as far as possible, requirements are described in terms that can be quantified and measured. The aim is to produce a statement of requirements sufficient for the definition of Business System Options in Step 210 (Define Business System Options).

The User Catalogue is developed to document all users that will be impacted by the new system.

Step 140: Investigate Current Data

This Step produces a model of the data that supports the current services. The development of the model uses information gathered for Step 115 (Develop Business Activity Model), Step 120 (Investigate and Define Requirements) and proceeds in parallel with Step 130 (Investigate Current Processing).

The data model represents only the data required to support the business activities on the Business Activity Model and processing defined in the Current Physical Data Flow Diagrams. The Elementary Process Descriptions supporting the Current Physical Data Flow Diagrams are used to validate that the data model does support the current processing. At this point it is not necessary to define all the attributes for each entity.

Step 150: Derive Logical View of Current Services

The Current Physical Data Flow Diagrams are converted into a logical view by removing the physical aspects of the current implementation. The revised Data Flow Diagrams represent the logical information system embedded in the current physical environment.

Although the removal of physical constraints may resolve some of the current problems identified, the extension of the Data Flow Diagrams to resolve outstanding problems and incorporate new requirements is not done until Step 310 (Define Required System Processing). The Current Environment Logical Data Model is validated to ensure it still supports the current processing. A formal cross-reference between entities on the Current Environment Logical Data Model and data stores on the Logical Data Flow Model is developed.

During logicalisation, requirements should be documented in the Requirements Catalogue.

12.2   Stage 2: Business System Options

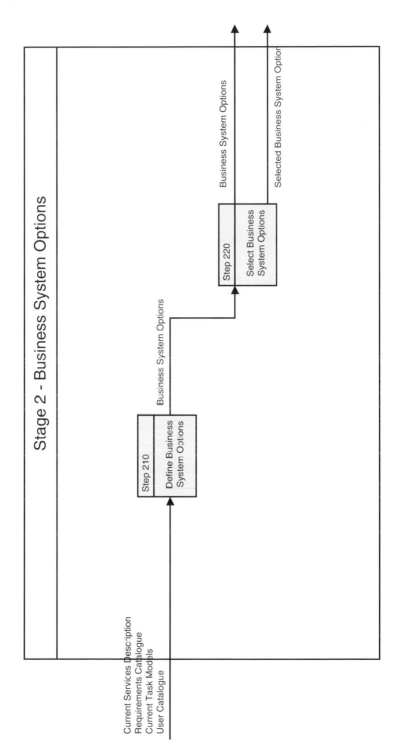

Stage 2 - Business System Options

Current Services Description
Requirements Catalogue
Current Task Models
User Catalogue

Step 210
Define Business System Options

Business System Options

Step 220
Select Business System Options

Business System Options

Selected Business System Option

To help management make a sound choice, carefully prepared options describing the scope and functionality of alternative ways of taking development and implementation further forward are constructed. They are optionally supported by technical documentation such as the Business Activity Model, Current Task Models, Logical Data Models and Data Flow Models. They also require financial and risk assessments to be prepared, and need to be supported by outline implementation descriptions. It is also the opportunity to define interfaces with other projects and business areas, particularly when the project is one of several in a large programme designed to keep projects to sizes which are more manageable.

Step 210: Define Business System Options

The Business System Options created in this Step are possible logical solutions to the users' requirements. Each option includes a description of its boundary, inputs, outputs, and some description of what happens within it.

This Step is concerned with identifying a number of possible system solutions, and developing two or three of those for presentation to the project board. There is no single 'correct' solution – invariably there are many possible systems which could be developed, differing in terms of functionality, impact on the organisation, and with different cost/benefit profiles. The project board must select the combination of elements which will best suit the requirements as perceived at the time. In some projects the view of possible functional choices may be significantly different from that envisaged in the Project Initiation Document. Indeed, this Step provides a vital opportunity to re-evaluate and to change the proposals made earlier, including the system boundary and the scope of the requirements.

Step 220: Select Business System Option

This Step completes the Requirements Analysis Module and is concerned with the presentation of the Business System Options to the project board and the selection of the preferred option. The selected Business System Option defines the boundary of the system to be developed in the Requirements Specification Module.

It may be necessary to make presentations to a wider audience than the project board to canvass opinions and promote acceptance and commitment. The selected option is often a hybrid of more than one option, including suggestions made during the presentation and selection process. The base option definition is therefore amended to describe the requirement in sufficient detail to define the scope of the required system.

12.3 Stage 3: Definition of Requirements

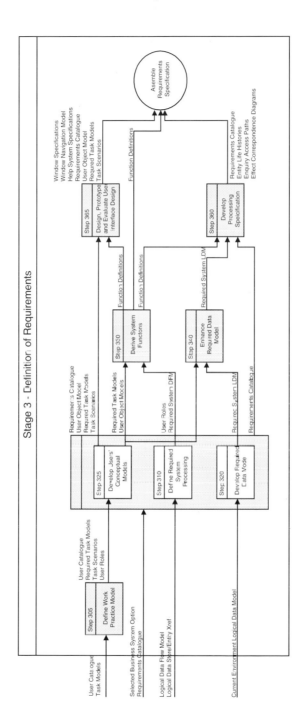

The Analysis of Requirements is reviewed to take account of the selected Business System Option using requirements definition, Data Flow Modelling and Logical Data Modelling techniques to adjust the Requirements Catalogue, data, user interface and process models and to expand their detail.

The Data Flow Diagrams are subsequently transformed into functions. The Logical Data Model is enriched and validated by Relational Data Analysis and Entity Life History Analysis. Events are specified in detail, and defined in terms of Effect Correspondences. These and the Enquiry Access Paths give a detailed set of access requirements to fully underpin the Logical Data Model.

The User Object Model is developed and used to develop the user Interface Design.

Step 305: Define Work Practice Model

Following the selection of the Business System Option, the users' Current Task Models are modified into the Required Task Models to match the new scope of the system. The Required Task Models will then be used as input into the derivation of the User Object Model in Step 325.

The User Catalogue, Task Scenarios and User Roles should also be developed within this step.

Step 310: Define Required System Processing

This Step is undertaken in parallel with Steps 320 and 325. The Requirements Catalogue is updated to reflect any changes that have been decided during the formulation and selection of Business System Options. The Logical Data Flow Model is used as the basis for the Required System Data Flow Model which reflects the new system as described in the selected Business System Option. The contents of data flows crossing the system boundary are fully defined and documented as I/0 Descriptions.

User roles are identified in this Step, for subsequent use during Dialogue Design. They are mapped to the Business Activity Model and organisation structure to develop an initial Work Practice Model.

Step 320: Develop Required Data Model

This Step is undertaken in parallel with Steps 310 and 325. The Logical Data Model of the current environment is extended to support the new requirements defined in the Requirements Catalogue and selected Business System Option. It is at this Step that entities and relationships are fully defined. Relevant non-functional requirements contained in the Requirements Catalogue are documented in the Logical Data Model.

Step 325: Develop Users' Conceptual Models

This step is undertaken in parallel with Steps 310 and 320. The Work Practice Model (output from Step 305) is used to develop the User Object Model which shows how the users view the objects within the new system.

As the Required Task Models and Task Scenarios are used here these can be changed by this step.

Step 330: Derive System Functions

This Step initially uses the Required System Data Flow Model, the Required Task Model, the User Object Model and the Requirements Catalogue to identify on-line and off-line functions. Functions are also identified with reference to events and enquiries identified and documented in the Event and Enquiry Catalogue. Events and enquiries can be identified from functions.

During the parallel definition of data and processing, additional events are identified, which cause existing functions to be updated, and new functions to be defined. Function Definition is not, therefore, regarded as complete until the end of Step 360 (Develop Processing Specification).

Step 340: Enhance Required Data Model

This Step uses the Relational Data Analysis techniques to validate the Required System Logical Data Model produced in Step 320.

The input and output data items are specified for each function in Step 330. These specifications can be used as the sources for Relational Data Analysis. Required forms or screen formats may also be used as inputs to Relational Data Analysis. Only a selection of the system's inputs and outputs are used as it is unnecessary and impractical to normalise all inputs and outputs. The normalised relations are used to build individual data sub-models which are then compared to the existing Logical Data Model. The resolution of structural differences is a matter of judgement, based on a knowledge of the present and likely future processing requirements.

Step 360: Develop Processing Specification

This Step is principally concerned with defining the detailed update and enquiry processing for the required system, previously only described in outline by the data flow diagrams. Logical Data Modelling and Behaviour Modelling are the major analysis and design tools in SSADM, leading the analyst to a thorough and more detailed understanding of the system. Entity Behaviour Modelling as an analysis tool raises detailed questions about how the system is to work, and in doing so completes the Required System Logical Data Model. As a design tool it produces, via Effect Correspondence Diagrams, a specification of the database update processing, which is completed in the Logical Design

Stage. Similarly, the development of Enquiry Access Paths forms the basis for the design of enquiries.

An initial set of events is identified during Business System Options and Function Definition. Since further events are identified during this Step, these may result in the creation of new functions or the modification of existing functions.

Step 365: Design, Prototype and Evaluate User Interface Design

This Step is concerned with the production of the User Interface Design which includes the Window Specifications, The Window Navigation Model and the Help System Specification. This Step is undertaken in parallel with Step 360.

Prototyping and Evaluation can be utilised within this Step to help specify the User Interface Design products.

As the conclusion of this Step all aspects of the user interface should be specified.

12.4   Stage 4: Technical System Options

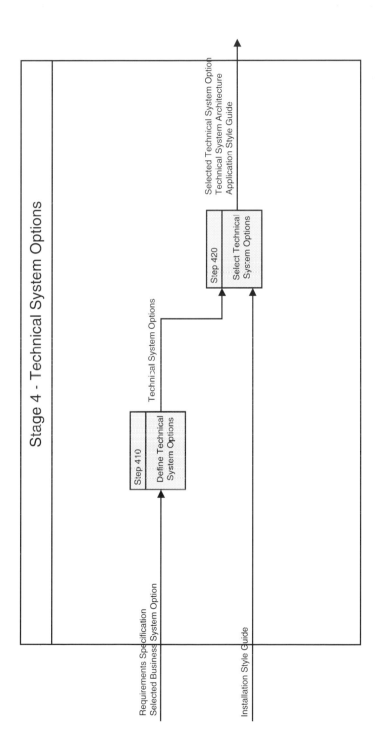

Several Technical System Options are developed, possibly including the 'no change' option. It is important at this point to determine how many are required, based on the parameters of the cost of producing each one to a useful level of detail, the need to demonstrate practicality, and the scope for exploring alternative approaches.

Detail can then be added in terms of costings, performance and impact on the organisation. The detailed options are then prepared for presentation.

The selection of the Technical System Option must involve management with the authority to authorise the expenditure, for it is their assessment of value for money which is the most critical.

Once the Technical System Option is selected, there is a need to consolidate the documentation into a Technical System Architecture for use in the Physical Design Stage.

Step 410: Define Technical System Options

The options created in this Step describe possible physical implementations to meet the Requirements Specification.

The Feasibility Study will have identified any major decisions already made in respect of hardware and software as a result of an IS Strategy (e.g., mainframe, mini-computer, or micro-computer; DBMS or conventional files). These will be reflected in the Requirements Catalogue; constrain the generic technical aspects of the Business System Option; and hence further constrain the Technical System Options. If they are not already in place, major hardware and software policies will need to be agreed with the project board in advance of this Step.

In some circumstances, particularly turnkey procurement, it may only be possible to nominate, and not define, the shape of the hardware/software environment. Then the description of the technical environment would be restricted to identifying the major constraints on the potential system such as location of peripherals, performance requirements and volumetrics.

The Technical System Options may also include possible variations on the system functionality specified in the Selected Business System Option as a result of more detailed analysis, cost/benefit information, or technical investigation.

Step 420: Select Technical System Options

This Step is concerned with the presentation of the Technical System Options to the project board and the selection of the preferred option. The Technical System Architecture of the selected Technical System Option sets the context for the Physical Design Module.

It may be necessary to make presentations to a wider audience than the project board to canvass opinions and promote acceptance and commitment. The selected option is often a hybrid based on one, but containing features from others.

The selected option is documented in the Technical System Architecture, which is carried forward to physical design.

12.5   Stage 5: Logical Design

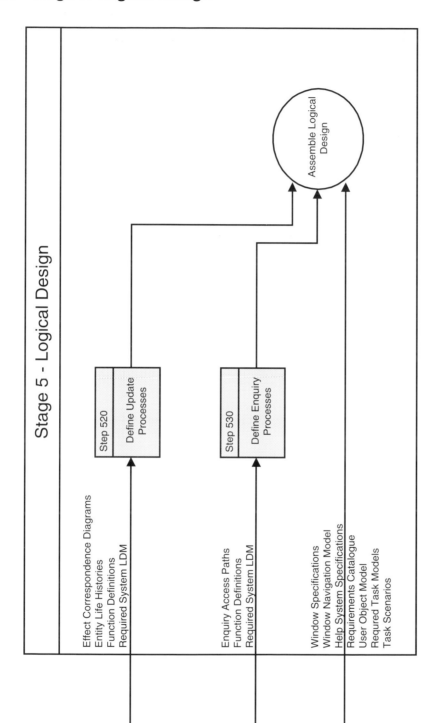

The information associated with updates (entity lives, effect correspondences) are transformed into update process specifications. That, associated with enquiries (access paths), becomes a set of enquiry process specifications. Especial care is given at this point to specifying error handling in all cases. In the case of Update Processing, state indicator values and their meanings are appended to the Logical Data Model.

The three components of the logical design are then assembled into a reviewed whole and submitted to management.

Step 520: Define Update Processes

This Step completes the logical specification of event processes. In Stage 3, the required database updates for each event are defined for each entity. At this point the defined entity updates are consolidated into a single processing structure for each event.

Taking each event in turn, the Effect Correspondence Diagram developed in Step 360 is developed into a single processing structure for the event.

Step 530: Define Enquiry Processes

This Step completes the logical specification of enquiries. Enquiries will have been defined at Stage 3 in terms of a data access path (Enquiry Access Path). At this point, a single processing structure for the enquiry is developed.

12.6   Stage 6: Physical Design

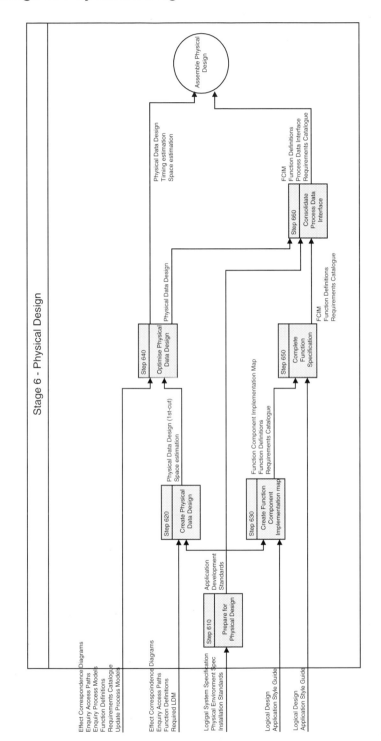

Physical Design addresses the following activities:

- prepare for Physical Design:
  - learn the rules of the implementation environment;
  - review the precise requirements for logical to physical mapping;
  - plan the approach.
- complete the specification of functions;
- incrementally and iteratively develop the data and process designs, using a cycle of:
  - design;
  - test against objectives;
  - optimise;
  - review.

This Stage has two main strands: data and processing. Initially, the physical environment is classified by the facilities and features it provides for both data and processing.

Within the data strand an initial Physical Data Design is produced, using rules of thumb applicable to any DBMS or file handler. This is converted to a product-specific data design. Timing and sizing is carried out on this design and, if necessary, changes made to the design to meet performance and space objectives.

A Physical Design Strategy is developed. This includes a definition, for the physical environment, of how process specification is to be approached and a definition of the style of program specifications.

The Physical Design procedures are intended to be used in conjunction with the product specific guides provided by suppliers.

Step 610: Prepare for Physical Design

The Physical Environment Classification scheme is used to categorise the physical environment, as described in the Physical Environment Specification. The classification scheme identifies the significant kinds of facility which implementation products can be expected to provide. It covers data storage, performance and processing system characteristics. How these facilities are supported in the physical environment clearly has an effect on the design of the system. The physical environment is classified according to the method(s) by which these facilities are provided. There are two main issues to address in the Processing System Classification. The first is how much of the physical processing can or should be specified in a non-procedural fashion. The second is how far the logical processes can be directly implemented as physical programs, or modules, within the physical system.

The Application Development Standards are defined. There are three main tasks in the definition of the Application Development Standards:

- the definition of the standards for the use of the physical processing system;

- the definition of the program specification standards, i.e., the format of the program specifications;

- the development of Activity Descriptions for the Physical Design activities that are specific to the implementation environment.

If a product-specific guide exists, it will contain most of the information required. However, some of the activity within this Step may still be necessary to understand and evaluate options presented in the interface guide.

Step 620: Create Physical Data Design

The Required System Logical Data Model is converted via a series of transformations into a first-cut Physical Data Design.

The strategy for producing the first-cut data design will have been defined in the Physical Design Strategy by identifying which facilities in the DBMS are to be taken advantage of, and the means of minimising the imposed constraints.

Initially the Required System Logical Data Model is converted into a Physical Data Design based on principles that are common to all database management systems. These determine the detailed requirements for physical data placement and performance. It is then converted to a product-specific design using the design rules specified in the Physical Design Strategy.

Step 630: Create Function Component Implementation Map

The components of each function which are not defined by the end of Stage 5 (syntax error handling; physical input/output formats; physical dialogues) are specified. The creation of the Function Component Implementation Map identifies duplicate and common function components, and defines the relationship between all the function components.

The components of functions that can be specified non-procedurally (in the particular physical environment) are defined to the physical processing system – with the exception of the database access components.

The specification of the database access components is deferred until Step 660 (Consolidate Process Data Interface) as part of the development of the Process Data Interface.

Step 640: Optimise Physical Data Design

The Physical Data Design is validated against the performance information contained in the Function Definitions and the Requirements Catalogue. This ensures earliest possible cross-validation of the two development streams. The Physical Data Design is optimised only if the preset performance objectives are not going to be achieved.

If there are any problems with meeting the space objectives the design is altered to overcome them. The system space objectives are defined in the Requirements Catalogue.

Timing forms are completed for the critical functions and the data design altered if necessary. This is done until performance objectives are met, a decision is made to alter the objectives, or it has become clear that the performance objectives can not be met solely by data design solutions.

Step 650: Complete Function Specifications

This Step is only undertaken if the components of the Function Component Implementation Map cannot be specified non-procedurally. If necessary, specific function models are produced to resolve outstanding structure clashes. Program specifications are produced for the function components requiring procedural code.

Step 660: Consolidate Process Data Interface

The Function Component Implementation Map data access components are compared with the optimised Physical Data Design to identify mismatches in 'views' of the data. The Function Component Implementation Map components will 'see' the database as the Required System Logical Data Model, but the Physical Data Design (for example, in a hierarchic DBMS) may have stored the data with other navigational routes. The mismatches are resolved by identifying first the keys and then the sequence of navigational steps required to deliver the Function Component Implementation Map components with its logical view of the data. This may be done non-procedurally using a data manipulation language such as SQL. In other cases, a specification for a procedural module is prepared according to installation standards and the approach decided in the Program Design Strategy.

The set of Process Data Interface components is then rationalised as with any other element of the Function Component Implementation Map and any special maintenance or enhancement requirements are recorded. The Requirements Catalogue may record performance requirements that are not able to be met by data design optimisation, and may need to be met by low-level routines in assembler-type language. Also recorded in this way are any syntax validation or other utilities using tool-specific features – automatic data dictionary validation facilities linked to screen painters, for example. All these tool-specific and special purpose utilities are catalogued together as the Process Data Interface to aid impact analysis, and to ensure version and product-specific features are visible to maintainers and enhancers. Any design compromises are recorded in the Requirements Catalogue against the requirements affected.

ANNEXE A - DESCRIPTION OF EU-RENT CASE STUDY

EU-Rent is a car rental company owned by EU-Corporation. It is one of three businesses – the other two being hotels and an airline – that each have their own business and IT systems, but share their customer base. Many of the car rental customers also fly with EU-Fly and stay at EU-Stay hotels.

EU-Rent business

EU-Rent has 1000 branches in towns all over Europe. At each branch cars, classified by car group, are available for rental. Each branch has a manager and booking clerks who handle rentals.

Rentals

Most rentals are by advance reservation; the rental period and the car group are specified at the time of reservation. EU-Rent will also accept immediate ('walk-in') rentals, if cars are available.

At the end of each day cars are assigned to reservations for the following day. If more cars have been requested than are available in a group at a branch, the branch manager may ask other branches if they have cars they can transfer to him/her.

Returns

Cars rented from one branch of EU-Rent may be returned to any other branch. The renting branch must ensure that the car has been returned to some branch at the end of the rental period. If a car is returned to a branch other than the one that rented it, ownership of the car is assigned to the new branch.

Servicing

EU-Rent also has service depots, each serving several branches. Cars may be booked for maintenance at any time provided that the service depot has capacity on the day in question.

For simplicity, only one booking per car per day is allowed. A rental or service may cover several days.

Customers

A customer can have several reservations but only one car rented at a time. EU-Rent keeps records of customers, their rentals and bad experiences such as late return, problems with payment and damage to cars. This information is used to decide whether to approve a rental.

Current IT system

Each branch and service depot has a local IT system based on PCs and a file server. The equipment is obsolete and limited in capacity (especially RAM). Hardware failures – screens, disk drives and power supplies – are increasingly frequent. There is currently no use of the Internet either for customer to business communication or for business to business communication.

Application maintainability

The application programs have been maintained over several years. Small RAM in the PCs has necessitated intricate, complex programs which makes amendments progressively more difficult and expensive.

Informal communication

Each location operates almost independently of others. Communication between locations is mainly by phone and fax and co-ordination is very variable. Sometimes, when a car is dropped off at a branch different from the pick-up branch, the drop-off branch will not inform the pick-up branch.

Branch managers tend to co-operate in small groups and not to look for 'spare' cars outside those groups. EU-Rent management feels that some capacity is wasted, but does not have reliable estimates of how much.

Scheduling of service bookings in branch and service depot files is co-ordinated by faxes between branch and depot. Sometimes service bookings are not recorded in the branch files, and cars booked for servicing are rented. Service depots sometimes do not get to know that a car has been transferred to a branch served by other depots until another depot requests the car's service history.

Customer blacklist

A copy of the customer blacklist is held at every branch. It should be updated every week from head office, but the logistics of updating the list with input from 1000 sources and sending out 1000 disks every week are beyond head office's capability. Updates are in fact sent out about every four weeks.

E-Commerce

There is no current use of e-commerce with customers having to phone or fax the individual offices to book cars for rental. This is causing problems in that some competitors have introduced facilities that enable customers to book and monitor their bookings over the Internet and it is thought that this is resulting in a loss of custom.

IT system replacement

EU-Rent management has decided that a new IT system is needed. It is expected whilst the basic operational activity is not expected to change significantly – locations and volume of rentals – it is expected that a number of 'online' systems (e.g. ordering of cars) will be implemented not necessarily as part of the initial role out but shortly thereafter. The new system is justified on three grounds:

- the current system cannot be kept going much longer;

- the perceived need to introduce some online system that can be accessed directly by customers over the Internet;

- better management of numbers of cars at branches and better co-ordination between branches is expected to increase utilisation of cars slightly – the same volume of business should be supportable with fewer cars. Each car ties up about 8,000 Euros in capital and loses about 3,000 Euros in depreciation, so significant savings are possible from small reductions in numbers of cars needed.

Corporate data

After the current IT system has been replaced, EU-Rent management wants to explore possibilities for sharing customer data across the car rental, hotel and airline systems. Even if customers are not stored in a single shared database, it makes sense for all three business areas to have consistent customer information on current address, telephone number, credit rating, etc.

It will be useful to know in each system when there are problems with a customer in other systems. And it may be possible to run promotions in one system, based on what EU-Corporation knows from the other systems about customers.

Future requirements

A customer loyalty incentive scheme is also under consideration. The requirement is not yet precisely defined but the scheme will be comparable with those offered by EU-Rent's competitors.

Members of the scheme will accumulate credit points with each car rental. They will exchange points for 'free' rentals. Only the base rental price will be payable by points; extra charges such as insurance and fuel will be paid for by cash or credit card. When this is introduced it is expected that customers will wish to be able to check (either by the use of a call-centre or directly over the Internet) the current state of their credit points.

Rationale for EU-Rent

The business of EU-Rent is car rentals, but this is largely irrelevant; it merely provides an easily understood context for examples. The business issues and user requirements in EU-Rent could be easily mapped to other systems. They include:

- a requirement to deliver a range of services (rental of cars of different quality and price) at many locations (rental branches), with different volumes of business and patterns of demand;

- customers who may use more than one location, but whose business with the whole organisation should be tracked;

- strong general policies set centrally (car models that may be used, rental tariffs, procedures for dealing with customers), but significant flexibility and authority for local managers (number of cars owned by branch, authority to over-ride published tariff to beat competitors' prices);

- a requirement for customers to be able to directly access aspects of the system;

- performance targets for local managers;

- a requirement for capacity planning and resource replenishment (disposal and purchase of cars, moving of cars between branches); possibilities for this to be managed locally, regionally or centrally;

- locally-managed sharing or swapping of resources or customers between branches to meet short-term unforeseen demand;

- an internal support structure (the maintenance depots) needed to maintain the resources and ensure that the product delivered to customers is of adequate quality;

- a customer base that is shared with other, separate systems (EU-Stay hotels and EU-Fly airline), and possibilities of communicating or co-ordinating with these systems.

Many of these characteristics are common to other types of business; for example, health care, vocational training, social security, policing, retail chain stores, branch banking.

ANNEXE B – GLOSSARY

3-Schema Specification Architecture

The Three-schema Specification Architecture has been introduced into the SSADM rationale as means of understanding the method's structure, in particular the distinction between the modelling of business rules, the user interface and the physical implementation of data management. This helps maintain a level of independence between the logical business requirements and the system implementation strategy, thus increasing the flexibility and robustness of the system design.

The Three-schema Specification Architecture divides the system design into three areas or 'views'.

- Conceptual Model;
- Internal Design;
- External Design.

Actor

A term used to identify a collection of proposed job holders who share a large proportion of common tasks, whether using the IT system or not.

ad-hoc enquiry

An enquiry which is not pre-defined but is created by the user as and when it is needed.

Application Development Standards

Defines the standards which apply to the physical design and development activities, for this project/application.

Application Naming Standards

Defines the naming conventions for all aspects of the application under development, with particular emphasis being placed on constraints imposed by the (physical) implementation environment.

Application Style Guide

Should be regarded as a set of standards, covering the user interface, to be followed within a particular application development. This document is based on the Installation Style Guide and tailored to the specific needs of a particular project.

Association

Is a relationship between two user objects, on a User Object Model, that the system will need to provide.

attribute

A characteristic property of an entity, or entity aspect, that is, any detail that serves to describe, qualify, identify, classify, quantify or express the state of an entity.

business activity

A transformation in the business system which acts on inputs to produce outputs. Business activities can be dependent on other business activities, they can be triggered by business events and are performed by actors in the business system. Business activities are the major components of a Business Activity Model. Where a business activity requires information support or is a candidate for automation, this will give rise to requirements in the Requirements Catalogue.

Business Activity Model

A Business Activity Model describes business activities, business events and business rules.

There is not a precise definition of what the Business Activity Model should look like. However, it should include:

- **Business Perspectives**; statement(s) of belief of what the business is trying to achieve;

- **Logical Activity Model;** what activities are carried out in the business and the dependencies between them; a distinction should be made between business and IS activities;

- **Business Events** and the business activities triggered when they occur;

- **Business Rules** – constraints and operational guidance – that determine how business activities are done.

Whatever approach has been used, the model may be validated by comparing it against a formal model of a Human Activity System as defined by Checkland.

business event

A business event is a trigger which activates one or more business activities.

Business events are of three types:

- external inputs – inputs from outside the system boundary;

- decisions made in business activities within the system;

- scheduled points in time.

A business event may trigger more than one activity. A business activity may be triggered by more than one business event. .

business perspective

Statement(s) of belief of what the business is trying to achieve. A single perspective can be shared by many different people and each person can subscribe to more than one perspective.

business rules

For many business activities there are explicit rules for how activities are done. Wherever rules are available, they should be referenced from the business activities. Rules are of two types – constraints and operational guidance.

Business System Options

The set of Business System Options which is compiled so that a selection can be made. The selected Business System Option is a description of a chosen system development direction. The description documents the system boundary, inputs, outputs and the transformation taking place within the boundary. Essentially the description is textual with supporting products such as Data Flow Diagrams.

business thread

A business thread can be recognised as the path through a set of business activities which are the outcome of an initiating business event. A thread does not need to be continuous in its progression, but may need further business events to trigger later business activities.

CASE tools

Computer-aided Software Engineering (CASE) tools are automated tools supporting
analysts in their use of design techniques. This type of tool normally supports the
diagrammatic techniques as well as containing a repository of information supporting the
diagrams.

candidate key

A candidate key is any (minimal) set of one or more attributes that can for all time be used
as a unique identifier of an entity or relation. 'Minimal' means that no subset of those
attributes identified as a candidate key is also a candidate key.

For each relation or entity, one candidate key must be selected as the primary key which is
used consistently throughout the system.

Capacity Planning

A technique used to predict the (hardware/software) configuration required to satisfy the
constraints and requirements of the proposed system.

It is also used to assist in the development of service level agreements.

character-based interface

Character-based interfaces rely on the use of a character set which is displayed on the
screen in a matrix of columns and rows. These character sets can include block graphic
characters which allow simple boxes to be drawn.

Conceptual Process Modelling

Is used to translate the information gathered during Entity Behaviour Modelling into a
logical specification of the required processing for events and enquiries which can then be
translated into a physical design for the system in any implementation. The precise
products of Conceptual Process Modelling may vary depending upon the technical
environment of the project.

Conceptual Process Modelling produces Effect Correspondence Diagrams, Enquiry Access
Paths, Update Process Models and Enquiry Process Models.

Context Diagram

A Data Flow Diagram consisting of a single process to represent the system and external entities to which information is given or information is received by the system. This may be drawn to illustrate the initial scope of the proposed system. The diagram concentrates on the major inputs and outputs of the system and shows the external sources and recipients of system data.

Current Environment Logical Data Model

Provides a detailed description of the information used or produced by the current environment. See also entries and Product Description for Logical Data Model.

Current Physical Data Flow Model

Shows how the current services are organised and processing is undertaken. An overview of current services is provided by documenting only the Level 1 Data Flow Diagram.

Database Design

Technique

Takes the Required System Logical Data Model and translates it into a product-specific database design within the chosen technical environment with consideration having been given to performance and space constraints.

Product

The definition for the physical database which is to be implemented. The design is developed in two steps; the first produces a 'first-cut' design based on applying rules about the DBMS to the Requires System Logical Data Model; the second is a design optimised for performance reasons.

Database Management System (DBMS)

The mechanism for managing data held within a computerised system. Conceptually data is held within one file regardless of how the content is physically organised.

data flow

Shows where data is being passed between different elements on a Data Flow Diagram. The name associated with the data flow should be meaningful to those reviewing the Data Flow Diagram.

Data flows will pass into and out of the system and between processes (generally via data stores except on the Current Physical Data Flow Model where process-to-process flows may reflect inadequacies in the current system). When the system boundary is being defined there may even be data flows between external entities.

At the lowest level of the Data Flow Diagram these are 'simple' data flows, though they may be combined into 'composite data flows' on higher level diagrams.

A data flow can be regarded as the data content of potential flows of data between elements of a Data Flow Diagram. Elementary data flows between elements on the bottom level diagrams may be aggregated in summary-level Data Flow Diagrams to form a hierarchy of data flows consistent with the hierarchy of DFD processes.

Data Flow Diagram (DFD)

A diagram representing the flow of information around a system, the way in which it is changed and stored and the sources and recipients of data outside the boundary of the system. Each Data Flow Diagram contains processes, data stores, external entities and data flows.

Data Flow Model (DFM)

A set of Data Flow Diagrams and their associated documentation. The diagrams form a hierarchy with the Data Flow Diagram Level 1 showing the scope of the system and the lower level diagrams expanding the detail as appropriate. Additional documentation provides a description of the processes, input/output data flows and external entities.

Data Flow Modelling

Is used to help define the scope of the system and ensure that the analysts have a clear understanding of the user's problems and requirements.

The technique is used to build a model of the information flows and not to define the detail of the processing performed by the system.

data item

Any element of data that is used within the system. Each data item may fulfil a number of different roles, each of which will be constrained by this central definition.

data store

A collection of any type of data in any form as represented on a Data Flow Diagram. In the Current Physical Data Flow Model, this may be a computer file or a box of documents or any other means of storing data.

Each data store is of one of the following types:

- **Main**. A repository of data which persists for a period of time. In the Logical and Required System Data Flow Models, a main data store represents a portion of the Logical Data Model. Each main data store must be composed of one or more entities;

- **Transient**. A type of data store which is temporary, accumulating data for use by another process when it is subsequently deleted. This data is not described within the Conceptual Model.

death

The state of an entity occurrence which no longer has an active role within the system. Entity occurrences can be interrogated by enquiries. Normally, the next state following death would be deletion.

Document Flow Diagram

Shows how documents pass around the system. This may be the initial diagram drawn within the Data Flow Modelling technique to assist in defining/identifying the boundary of the system. This diagram will be produced if the current system is predominantly clerical and involves the passing of information using forms or other documents.

effect

The set of processing initiated by an event for a single entity.

effect correspondence

A one-to-one relationship between effects. There are two types of correspondence represented by this concept:

- single - between two single effects;

- iterated between one single effect and a 'set of' another effect.

An effect correspondence is directional and will almost always represent an access via a relationship on the Logical Data Model. An effect may be the source of many correspondences but the destination of only one.

Effect Correspondence Diagram

Shows all the effects an event has on entities within the system and how those effects correspond to one other. Operations and conditions can be added to the diagrams to act as a complete specification of the processing required for an event. Where required, Effect Correspondence Diagrams may be transformed into Update Process Models.

Elementary Process Description

Each process at the lowest level of decomposition (i.e., which is indicated by an asterisk as being at the bottom level) is described by an Elementary Process Description (EPD).

An Elementary Process Description is a brief textual description of the process. This description may contain the following:

- what data is accessed;

- what business constraints dictate how the process is carried out;

- circumstances under which the process is invoked;

- constraints on when and by whom the process can be invoked.

enquiry

An element which requires information to be read from the Logical Data Model but involves no update processing. Some update functions contain enquiries as well as updates (events).

Enquiry Access Path

The route through the Logical Data Model from an entry point to the entity, or entities, required for a particular enquiry.

Enquiry Process Model

Consists of a Jackson-like structure diagram describing the processing required for an enquiry. The structure is based on the Enquiry Access Path.

entity

Something, whether concrete or abstract, which is of relevance to the system and about which information needs to be stored. This concept represents a general definition of the entity that can be shared by a number of different systems/ areas. It is the aspect of the entity relevant to the system under investigation that is represented within a specific project's Logical Data Model.

Entity Access Matrix

A grid that is used to identify which entities are affected by a particular event or accessed by specific enquiries. It provides two checks that is: that each event/enquiry affects/accesses at least one entity and that each entity is affected by at least one event.

Entity Description

Documents all of the details concerned with entities on the Logical Data Structure.

Entity Life History

An Entity Life History (ELH) charts all of the events that may cause a particular entity occurrence to change in some way and places them in sequence.

An Entity Life History is a combination of all possible lives for every occurrence of an entity. Each occurrence is constrained to act in the way defined by the Entity Life History for that entity.

event

An event is something that triggers a Conceptual Model process to update the system data. It is usually sourced by an event which occurs in the business environment, notified to the system via one or more functions. An event provides the reason for an update process to be initiated. The name of the event should reflect what is causing the process to be invoked and not the process name itself. Typical event names might include terms such as 'Receipt', 'Notification', 'Decision', 'Arrival', 'New', 'Change' event data

External Design

System Development Template element

The External Design comprises the user interface: data definitions for input/output files, screens and reports; process definitions for dialogue input/output programs. External Design depends on trade-offs between many factors, for example, ergonomics, system efficiency and users' various subjective preferences. This is a creative area and heuristic approaches, such as prototyping, can have a role here. The External Design passes event data and enquiry triggers to the Conceptual Model, and receives event and enquiry output in response.

external entity

Whatever or whoever donates data to or receives data from the system. Represented on Data Flow Diagrams as an oval. An external entity may be another system, an external file/database, an organisation, an individual or a group of people.

External Entity Description

Used to explain, briefly, the relevance of an external entity in relation to the existing or proposed system. The detail will cover responsibilities or functions of the external entity and any constraints on the interface with the proposed system.

Feasibility Report

This is the product which documents the possible approaches to the system development and assesses the impact of each so that the most appropriate way ahead can be fully investigated.

foreign key

A foreign key is defined as a non-key attribute (or group of related non-key attributes) in one relation or entity which is the same as the key of another relation or entity.

function

A user-defined packaging of events and enquiries and the processing they trigger that will be accessed from the External Design. Functions can be categorised as enquiry/update, off-line/on-line, user-initiated/system initiated. This volume covers only on-line functions.

Function Component Implementation Map (FCIM)

A classification and specification of all implementation fragments for all function components defined in the Function Definitions to meet the processing requirements.

Function Definition (technique)

For on-line functions Function Definition identifies units of processing specification, or functions, which package together the essential services of the system in the way required by the user organisation.

Function Definition (product)

The product of the Function Definition technique is a group product called the Function Definition. This is composed of the following products:

- Function Description;
- Function Navigation Model.

Function Description

The Function Description contains some descriptive text and a large number of cross-references to other products. The precise format of the product will depend upon the documentation tools available to the project.

Function Navigation Model

A model, constructed for complex functions, which shows how the different parts of the function relate to each other.

Graphical User Interface (GUI)

Graphical User Interfaces (GUIs) allow each dot or pixel on the screen to be addressed individually. Characters are made up of groups of pixels and can be made any size and in a variety of fonts. Graphic objects such as lines and arcs can be drawn. GUIs are almost always used in conjunction with windows, icons, a mouse and pop-up or pull-down menus.

Help System Specification

A description of the help system in terms of the procedures to be adopted for help and areas to be covered.

installation development standards

Input to Physical Design. Documents the criteria which should be used during the development of all Information Systems within the organisation/installation. Note precise details of the contents of this Product are not given within this volume set.

I/O Descriptions

Are used to document all data flows which cross the Data Flow Model system boundary. They list the data items contained in the data flows. Detail of the structure of the data – such as repeating groups and optionality – need not be included, since this will be rigorously defined on I/O Structures.

I/O Structure

Structure diagram representing data input to and output from functions. An I/O Structure consists of an I/O Structure Diagram optionally supported by an I/O Structure Element Description.

Internal Design

System Development Template element

The Internal Design defines the physical database design and the process/data interface. There is a dependency on trade-offs, between such factors as timing, space utilisation and maintainability. It is a creative area where there is no 'right' answer. Heuristic approaches may be appropriate.

Logical Data Flow Model

A variant of Data Flow Model.

A logical model of the current services, free of physical or organisational constraints. The Logical Data Flow Model is created from the Current Physical Data Flow Model, by carrying out specific activities. The aim is to remove duplication in processing and data stores, and to re-group bottom-level processes into the functional areas that the user requires.

Logical Data Model

Provides an accurate model of the information requirements of all or part of an organisation. This serves as a basis for file and database design, but is independent of any specific implementation technique or product.

Logical Data Modelling

Logical Data Modelling is used to investigate and model the structured data that is held within a system as information support to business activities. The technique is used to both model the data of the current system and to build a model of what are the data requirements of the new system.

Logical Data Modelling is at the very heart of nearly all projects.

Logical Data Store/Entity Cross-reference

Is a product showing the correspondence between logical data stores in the Logical or Required System Data Flow Model and the entities on the Logical Data Model. This is used to ensure that a main data store corresponds to an entity or group of entities. Also each entity on the Logical Data Model must be held completely within one and only one main data store on the Logical or Required System Data Flow Model. (Transient data stores are not included in the Logical Data Store/Entity Cross-reference)

Logical Data Structure

A diagrammatic representation of the information needs of an organisation in the form of entities and the relationships between them.

The Logical Data Structure formalises the structure of information by depicting diagrammatically the different types of relationship in which entities can participate.

A Logical Data Structure consists of two basic components:

- entities;
- relationships.

menu

A hierarchical structure used to provide a user (role) with access to available, and applicable functions.

Menu Structure

Provides a diagrammatic representation of the menus to be used within the system.

Normal Form

Is the result of applying the Relational Data Analysis technique to groupings of data input to or output from the system. There are several stages of normalisation; relations are translated into:

- First Normal Form (1NF)
- Second Normal Form (2NF)
- Third Normal Form (3NF)

off-line function

A function where all the data is input and the whole of the database processing for the function is completed without further interaction with the user.

on-line function

A function where the system and the user communicate through input and output messages, i.e., message pairs. The system responds in time to influence the next input message. On-line functions may include off-line elements such as printing an off-line report.

operation

An elementary piece of processing.

parallel structure

Appearing on Entity Life Histories, this is used to show where certain events will definitely happen within the lifetime of an entity, but not in a prescribed order.

Physical Design Strategy

Documents all aspects relating to designing the physical implementation of the system.

Physical Environment Classification

Classifies the environment in which the application is to be implemented. Also describes the development environment and migration path where necessary.

Physical Environment Specification

Specifies the hardware and software products and services to be supplied, commissioned and made available for implementation. Generally this will be provided by the vendor.

Physical Process Specification

Packages all of the specifications for processing which are required in the proposed system. This is sometimes known as Program Specifications.

Process Data Interface

Documents how the Logical Data Model can be mapped onto the Physical Data Design, showing how it interfaces with the Physical Processing Specification. It allows the designer to implement the logical update and enquiry processes as physical programs, independently of the physical database structure.

primary key

A primary key is an attribute or a combination of attributes which can be used to uniquely identify an entity or relation.

Primary Task Model

The Primary Task Model of a Human Activity System defines what the system does in order to be the one defined in the Root Definition. The Primary Task Model is a coherent set of connected activities.

A Primary Task Model is derived formally from its Root Definition, and only from its Root Definition. It should not include any real-world activities that are not represented in the Root Definition.

Product Description

Describes the purpose, form and components of a product, and lists the quality criteria which apply to it.

process

Transforms or manipulates information (data) in a system. Appears within a Data Flow Model. Can be hierarchically decomposed.

project

A project is regarded as having the following characteristics:

- a defined and unique set of technical products to meet the business needs;
- a corresponding set of activities to construct those products;
- a certain amount of resources;
- a finite and defined lifespan;
- an organisational structure with defined responsibilities.

prototype

Provides the user with an animated view of how the system being developed will work. It enhances user understanding, allowing better identification of discrepancies and deficiencies in the user requirement. It can used as part of incremental development.

quality criteria

Characteristics of a product which determine whether it meets requirements, and thus define what 'quality' means in the context of that product. These are defined in the Product Descriptions and agreed with the project board before development of the product commences.

quit and resume

The use of Quit and Resume helps the analyst separate out alternative patterns in an Entity Life History, each of which starts the same way. Quits and Resumes are used to jump from an 'assumed case' to an 'alternative case'. The assumed case is always visited first on the Entity Life History. When an event occurs which shows that the Entity Life History should be in the alternative case, a quit occurs to the appropriate part of the alternative case.

Required System Data Flow Model

A variant of the Data Flow Model which represents the new system without any physical constraints but structured around the user's view of the system.

Requirements Catalogue

Is the central repository for information covering all identified requirements, both functional and non-functional. Each entry is textual and describes a required facility or feature of the proposed system.

Relational Data Analysis

Is a method of deriving data structures which have the least redundant data and the most flexibility. The flexibility is achieved by breaking down the data groups into smaller groups without losing any of the original information. It is the objective of this technique to transform all relations into at least third normal form.

'Normalisation' uses rules to analyse the way items of data depend upon one another for their meaning.

In a 'normalised Logical Data Model' all entities, considered as relations, must be in third (or higher) normal form.

relationship

Is an association between two entities (entity aspects), or one entity (aspect) and itself (recursion/involution), to which all instances (occurrences) of the relationship must conform.

Relationship Description

Documents the details of a relationship between two entities on the Logical Data Structure. Part of the Logical Data Model.

Required System Logical Data Model

Provides the detail of the proposed system information requirements. It is developed during the Requirements Specification and Logical System Specification Modules. It is compared with the results of Relational Data Analysis to produce a normalised model.

See also Logical Data Model.

state indicator

Each entity has a state indicator, updated each time an event causes an update to the entity's data. A state indicator can be thought of as an additional attribute within each entity. Where there is a need to record that an event has occurred, the state indicator is automatically updated to a new value.

Style Guide

A guide which shows how to implement various elements of the user interface. Style Guides are of great importance in projects to ensure a common look and feel across all the facilities within the application.

There are two main types of style guide:

- the Installation Style Guide, which sets broad standards for all applications within the organisation as a whole;

- the Application Style Guide, which is an elaboration of the Installation Style Guide for use on a particular project.

sub-type

An entity representing a particular alternative behaviour of the corresponding super-type entity. A sub-type contains all the attributes which are specific to that sub-type only. Sub-types of the same super-type are always alternatives of each other.

super-type

An entity which has several different alternative behaviours such that each occurrence of the entity is of a particular type.

System Development Template

The System Development Template provides a common structure for the overall system development process.

It divides the process into a number of distinct areas of concern:

- Investigation;
- Specification;
- Construction;
- Decision Structure;
- User Organisation;
- Policies and Procedures.

task

A human activity performed by an actor in response to a business event. The task is identified, from the 'human' perspective, with reference to all the business activities triggered by a specific business event which are undertaken by a single actor.

Task Model

A model which describes all of the human activities and task sequences required by the business system. The Task Model elaborate the tasks identified by the mapping of business activities onto the user organisation. Task Models tend to cover all the major tasks and a subset of the less common tasks. Task Models are documented as part of the Work Practice Model.

Technical System Architecture

Provides the specification of the technical environment which is produced once the Technical System Option has been selected. This detail is then passed on to physical design activities.

Technical System Options

The set of Technical System Options which has been developed so that the system development direction can be chosen.

Each option documents the functions to be incorporated and details implementation requirements. Each description is textual with some planning information. Functional elements are taken directly from the Requirements Specification

transient data store

Transient data is held for a short time before being used by a process and then deleted. Data held in transient data stores may not be structured in the same way as the data in a main data store.

Update Process Model

Is a structure diagram for the update (event) processing and the associated operations list. This is based on the Entity Life Histories, which provide a data-oriented view of the system, and the associated Effect Correspondence Diagrams, which provide an event-oriented or process-oriented view of the system.

User Catalogue

Provides a description of the on-line users of the proposed system. It includes details of job titles and the tasks undertaken by each of the identified users.

user

A person who will require direct interaction with the automated system.

user class

A subset of the total population of users of the required system who are similar in terms of their frequency of use, relevant knowledge and personal experience.

User Object

Something the user will want to recognise as a component of the user interface of the automated system. User Objects may represent a set of data, a computer system device or a container for other user objects. User Objects are modelled on the User Object Model.

User Object Model

A model made up of User Objects and Associations which is, in essence, a user's mental model of the structure and contents of the system. It would be usual to build a single User Object Model for the system which is used as a vital part of the design of the user interface.

user role

A collection of job holders who share a large proportion of common tasks or who have the same access security privileges for the system.

window

A communication channel through which the user looks to view and interact with elements of the automated system.

Window Navigation Model

A model which describes the window and dialogue structure and how the user navigates between windows.

Window Specifications

A specification which describes how the window will look in terns of views, states and actions. The specifications can be produced textually or as part of a prototype.

Work Practice Model

This is the mapping of business activities and scheduling constraints onto an Organisation Structure. This requires the definition of user roles and classification of users (derived from User Analysis) so that business activities can be assigned to 'actors'.

INDEX

A

action
        User Interface Design and 48
        User Object Modelling and 42
Activity Network 80
actors
        definition of 144
        Work Practice Modelling and 39
ad-hoc enquiry 144
application characteristics 89
Application Development Standards 67, 144
Application Naming Standards 144
Application Style Guide 145
association
        description of 145
        User Object Modelling and 42
assumptions, default SSADM 87–8
attribute
        description of 145
        Logical Data Model, concept of 21
automated systems
        business activities on 94–5
        interaction mode between users and 96
        interfaces with other 96–7

B

basic task, Work Practice Modelling 39
Behaviour Modelling *see* Entity Behaviour
  Modelling
bureaucracy, avoidance of 85
business activities
        assignment to user organisations 95–6
        automation of 94–5
        Business Activity Modelling, concept of
          16
        description of 145
        SSADM and support of the 7–8
        Three-schema Specification Architecture,
          relationship between 9–10
Business Activity Model
        basis for Business System Option 94–7
        description of 145–6

        Logical Data Model and 24
        purpose of 16
        supporting business activity 7–8
Business Activity Modelling
        Business System Option and 102
        concepts of 16
        Data Flow Modelling and 34
        Entity Behaviour Modelling and 58
        interrelationship to other SSADM
          techniques/products 18
        overview of 16–18
        products of 17
        Requirements Definition and 20
Business Context 15–20
business events 16, 17, 145, 146
business perspectives 16, 145, 146
business risks 81
business rules 16, 17, 145, 146
Business Sustem Development series,
  organisation of techniques within 2
Business System Option
        automation of business activities 94–5
        Business Activity Model, derivation from
          94–7
        common features of options 98
        cost/benefit analysis 99
        coverage of options 97–8
        delivery scheduling 99–100
        description of 146
        development of each 97–100
        documenting the selection 101
        interaction mode, user and automated
          system 96
        interfaces to other systems 98
        interfaces with other automated
          systems/resources 96–7
        making the selection 101
        organisation and user roles, description
          of 99
        overview of 92–102
        product of 93
        Requirements Definition and 20
        selection considerations 100–101
        steps towards selection 100
        technical considerations 99
        Technical System Options and 114
        technique for 93–101
        textual description 93